on track ...

Earth, Wind and Fire

every album, every song

Bud Wilkins

T0243782

sonicbondpublishing.com

Sonicbond Publishing Limited
www.sonicbondpublishing.co.uk
Email: info@sonicbondpublishing.co.uk

First Published in the United Kingdom 2023
First Published in the United States 2023

British Library Cataloguing in Publication Data:
A Catalogue record for this book is available from the British Library

Typeset in ITC Garamond & ITC Avant Garde
Printed and bound in England

Graphic design and typesetting: Full Moon Media

Follow us on social media:
Twitter: https://twitter.com/SonicbondP
Instagram: https://www.instagram.com/sonicbondpublishing_/
Facebook: https://www.facebook.com/SonicbondPublishing/

Linktree QR code:

Dedications

Thanks to everyone whose ear I've talked off during the trial and tribulations of writing this book! Extra love to my partner and the best of all, Leilani Le Fleur, for being everything and helping me with everything else. You're too awesome. A million thanks to my mum Kathy for being the most amazing person ever, my dad Carey for being so cool, my brother Matt and his family - always ready to talk about anything from Kevin Sullivan to Bob Willis, and my brother Jason and his family. My besties Matt Witton and Matt Furlani; always a pleasure old chaps. Everyone I get to play guitar to, and that I work the stage with. The goodest boy in the whole world Blakey, you sat with me during every second of writing this, and I now know for sure that there is none with a hairier neck than thou.

Last but definitely not least, thanks a million to Stephen Lambe and Sonicbond Publishing for opening this door.

Would you like to write for Sonicbond Publishing?

At Sonicbond Publishing we are always on the look-out for authors, particularly for our two main series:

On Track. Mixing fact with in depth analysis, the On Track series examines the work of a particular musical artist or group. All genres are considered from easy listening and jazz to 60s soul to 90s pop, via rock and metal.

On Screen. This series looks at the world of film and television. Subjects considered include directors, actors and writers, as well as entire television and film series. As with the On Track series, we balance fact with analysis.

While professional writing experience would, of course, be an advantage the most important qualification is to have real enthusiasm and knowledge of your subject. First-time authors are welcomed, but the ability to write well in English is essential.

Sonicbond Publishing has distribution throughout Europe and North America, and all books are also published in E-book form. Authors will be paid a royalty based on sales of their book.

Further details are available from www.sonicbondpublishing.co.uk. To contact us, complete the contact form there or email info@sonicbondpublishing.co.uk

on track ...

Earth, Wind and Fire

Contents

Introduction

> Being joyful and positive was the whole objective of the group. Our goal was to reach all the people and to keep a universal atmosphere, to create positive energy. All of our songs had that positive energy. To create uplifting music was the objective.
> Maurice White

So intertwined are Earth, Wind & Fire with contemporary music, so deeply do their songs rouse us from negativity and attach to positive life memories, it's almost impossible to imagine modern pop music without their input. It's arguable that their hits were so all-encompassing, the group have been overlooked when conversations about the greatest acts have taken place. Earth, Wind & Fire *are* somewhat taken for granted, but the reality is that they – originally led fearlessly by Maurice White – are undoubtedly one of the greatest groups of all time. Their hits start instant parties no matter where in the world they are heard. Their soaring ballads – and the incendiary voice of Philip Bailey – can take you away to wherever they want you to be. When the group is firing on all cylinders, it's indescribable.

EW&F redefined funk, rhythm and blues, pop and disco, though as musicians, they were most comfortable with the description of fusion players making pop music. They infused everything they touched with a deep spiritualism that became their calling card. The group's identity as strong black men living in America (and all that that entails), pervaded their output – their pride shining through in the music, artwork, stage shows and costumes. They boldly blended elements of Afrofuturism into their music, unflappable in their self-belief.

The story begins with the birth of band leader and visionary Maurice White in Memphis, Tennessee, on 19 December 1941. White's Pentecostal upbringing and experiences with gospel music were to guide his music for his entire life. As a child, he made friends with future organ-playing legend Booker T. Jones, and gravitated towards the drum kit as his primary means of expression. Upon graduating high school, Maurice headed for Chicago and Crane Junior College, where he met future bandmates Louis Satterfield (bass/trombone) and Don Myrick (saxophone). Maurice's percussion style scored him the attention of Vee-Jay Records and launched his early career as a session musician. Betty Everett's hit 'You're No good' was one of his first sessions, and he began working his way up the ladder until a successful audition for the Chess Records house band led to a true breakthrough. Playing on a large amount of classic Chess Records material would be enough to put any drummer on the short-list of greats, but this was just the tip of White's iceberg. His rhythms were heard behind such Chess luminaries as Chuck Berry, Muddy Waters, Etta James and many more – White's most legendary session performance perhaps being the Fontella Bass classic 'Rescue Me'.

Meanwhile, unknowingly planting seeds for the future, Maurice was returning home with stacks of Chess records for his family, including younger brothers Fred and Verdine. Fred had taken to the drums at a very young age – to mimic his older brother – and Verdine soon discovered music for himself. Maurice began seeking opportunities away from Chess, and became the drummer for jazz pianist Ramsey Lewis. Playing on some of Lewis' biggest hits – including his version of the spiritual 'Wade In The Water' – White's future group was to be associated with the jazz pioneer. White remembered in his autobiography *My Life With Earth, Wind & Fire:* 'I learned everything from Ramsey, from the mundane to the complex – have extras of anything and everything possible; know the music stores in each city, just in case you need one. Next to the performance itself, sound and lighting checks were the most important part of our day'.

Around this time, Maurice's interest in astrology and spiritualism began to play a bigger part in his life, becoming a main theme in his later work. He contacted Chicago's leading astrologer, who, upon learning Maurice's birthplace and time, announced that he had no water sign in his chart: only earth, air and fire. Maurice was also introduced to the traditional African instrument, the kalimba. The sound mesmerised him, and he imagined merging traditional instruments with modern musical styles.

Verdine and Fred White were developing on their instruments with incredible speed. Verdine took lessons from double-bassist Radi Velah of the Chicago Symphony Orchestra, and simultaneously learnt about the electric bass from Chess session player Louis Satterfield. Fred soon became an in-demand session drummer, and was snatched up by Maurice's old friend Donny Hathaway – Fred's first tour performances being captured on Hathaway's *Live* album (1972).

Merging with vocalist Wade Flemons and keyboardist/bassist Don Whitehead, Maurice started Salty Peppers. Their debut recording – the single 'La La Time' – included younger brother Fred on percussion, and Donny Hathaway on keys, while also providing vocal arrangements. Though 'La La Time' stalled in Chicago, Maurice kept on pushing, and Capitol Records in Los Angeles eventually picked up the single and turned it into a minor hit. This inspired White to put it all on the line and leave behind his Chess session work and high-paying job with Ramsey Lewis. Maurice invited a group of musicians, including Flemons, Whitehead, percussionist Yackov Ben Israel and Verdine to move to Los Angeles on the premise of Capitol extending their contract. The lineup was completed with guitarist Michael Beal, trombonist Alex Thomas, saxophonist Chester Washington and trumpeter Leslie Drayton. Maurice christened the group Earth, Wind and Fire after the words of his astrologer, swapping the air for wind simply because he liked the sound more and felt the word implied the same element. Unfortunately, in a big blow, Capitol decided against signing the group. But undeterred, Maurice began networking his way into the L.A. music scene, rehearsing his band constantly. All the pieces were in place for Earth, Wind & Fire to begin on their path.

Earth, Wind And Fire (1971)

Personnel:
Maurice White: vocals, drums, electric kalimba
Verdine White: vocals, bass, percussion
Don Whitehead: vocals, piano
Yackov Ben Israel: percussion
Michael Beal: guitar
Sherry Scott: vocals
Wade Flemons: vocals, electric piano
Chester Washington: tenor saxophone
Alexander Thomas: trombone
Leslie Drayton: trumpet
Producer: Joe Wissert
Engineer: Bruce Botnick
Studio: Sunset Sound Recorders, Hollywood
Release date: February 1971
Chart positions: US soul: 24, UK: -
Running time: 28:34

The debut album shows the band in fine form but miles away from the pop/
funk phenomenon they were to become. Augmenting the band is Sherry
Scott, whose bluesy vocal style sat well in the vocal section of Maurice,
Verdine, Don Whitehead and Wade Flemons. With the lineup complete, the
band constantly rehearsed, turning themselves into a tight funk machine.
Maurice remembered the early shows in his autobiography: 'Since we
rehearsed all the time, everything we did was tight. Verdine pranced around
in a leotard and no shirt, giving a good show. Our driving, percussive sound
created high energy and raw musical power'.

Maurice had been networking and making friends in high places. Legendary
NFL player Jim Browne organised a showcase for Warner Bros. and RCA
Records atop his Hollywood Hills mansion. Overlooking the L.A. horizon,
the group played their best. RCA turned them down, but Warner Bros.
immediately saw potential and snatched up the group. To produce the first
project, the label chose Joe Wissert, who was fresh from working with The
Turtles and Gordon Lightfoot. Wissert went on to produce multiple EW&F
albums, and worked with artists like Boz Scaggs, Helen Reddy and the J.Geils
Band. The role of recording engineer fell to Bruce Botnick – most famous for
his groundbreaking work with The Doors.

Sounding today like a lost garage-funk classic, due partly to its warm
sound, the album is still looked upon favourably – none other than R&B artist
Isaac Hayes having called it one of the group's top five records.

'Help Somebody' (White, Flemons, Whitehead)
Straight away, the group placed themselves amongst the up-tempo funk of the
day, and the opening track could be straight from an early-1970s car-chase

scene. Beginning with Beal's stabbing octave guitar line, the horn and rhythm sections join in, and before long, the song takes off. Beal's locked-in rhythm-playing anchors the James Brown-style vamp heard in the verse, while Wade Flemons holds the distinction of being the first voice we hear on an EW&F album. At first, joined by Maurice, vocalist Sherry Scott's appearance lifts the song, floating above a rhythm change that's similar to a samba.

The first hearing of bassist Verdine White on an EW&F album is a treat, and over the course of the 1970s, listeners really got to hear the growth of an amazing musician. Here, his playing is rock solid, driving the track forward in a way similar to bassist Larry Graham. The wall of percussion that helped shape the group's sound is present from the start, as are the complex vocal counter-melodies. This is evident in the layered vocal parts of the 'Reach out your hand' section. The lyric is fairly straightforward in its reinforcement of the title, urging the listener to 'Go out and help somebody else', reminding them to also 'Let love prevail/Reach out your hand and help somebody'.

'Moment Of Truth' (White, Flemons, Whitehead)
This intro brings the group's jazz influences to the fore. For a few moments, the horn section and drum rolls are reminiscent of a Duke Ellington intro (or ending, for that matter), and other big-band arrangers of the swing era. Verdine's sliding bass line quickly interrupts this, followed by a driving groove that the band stays locked into – the old making way for the new, perhaps? Beal uses a wah pedal extensively on this track – sometimes creatively and sometimes locked into the drums. The wall of percussion continues, the listener is hit by interlocking rhythms.

The multiple vocalists in unison, in harmony or solo, is particularly reminiscent of legendary funk group Sly Stone and the Family Stone. Over in Detroit, similar vocal arrangements were popping up on albums by the emerging group Funkadelic. Led by the inimitable George Clinton, Funkadelic were up to album number three by this stage, but their ascent would mirror that of EW&F in many ways. The verse and chorus fly by, broken up with a small section featuring vocal scatting. Soon, a new vocal hook appears over a repeat of the intro groove, with Scott establishing a memorable vocal pattern that would fit well with EW&F's future direction.

'Love Is Life' (White, Flemons, Whitehead)
This first EW&F soul ballad is possibly the album highlight. The late-1960s saw plenty of hits along these lines, but EW&F were eventually able to transcend what had come before and increase the complexity and sound for the 1970s and beyond – beginning right here.

'Love Is Life' was the album's highest-charting single, reaching 43 R&B in *Billboard*. A slow rhythm, jazz chords, and a flute added to the horn section, provide a bed for Scott's spoken intro. 'Love, the light shines, and through its wisdom, the answers of the universe are carried' are words that would today probably be described as being 'of their time', though they helped set the tone and were a precursor to the spiritual elements that would become an essential part of the EW&F image. The lyric itself is similar, with the horn section giving a melody preview before the unison vocals come in over the descending chords.

> Have you ever seen a flower
> Tryin' to bloom in a dry, barren land?
> But then comes a sweet, sweet shower
> Just to lend a helpin' hand

The verse's restrained feel is blown away by the pre-chorus, as the band steps it up and the horn stabs give the swelling vocals energy. The sliding singing style of 'all at once' sounds not unlike something from a later EW&F record. A quick-but-rousing chorus proclaiming 'You brought me love, and your love is life', has baritone sax holding down the bottom end before a drum buildup ends the section with a rising burst of horns.

The post-second-chorus section is important, as it's where the band begin to sound like themselves. The vocal and horn-section interaction is of particular interest. Bassists should note the section repeats as Verdine jumps high and applies a fast vibrato in a style that later became one of his signatures. We also hear guitarist Beal soloing, and as the song fades out, we are treated to what would become the tradition of impromptu talking between tracks, as an unknown voice (perhaps aware of the lyric's flower-power elements) mentions 'peace and love'.

'Fan The Fire' (White, Flemons, Whitehead)
The first track to include any social commentary is smouldering funk. The opening chant, 'The flame of love is about to die/Somebody fan the fire' sets the tone as horns creep in over the repetitive bass-and-drums rhythm. They soon give way to a strong mid-tempo groove, with great guitar work from Beal, whose intro solo immediately suggests he might attempt to steal the limelight. Maurice spoke of the lyric in his autobiography:

> Don Whitehead's vibe was a big part of these songs. 'Head' was more curious about world events than Wade and I – aware of what was going on with (Black Panther founding members) Bobby Seale, Huey Newton, and even the work of (poet/activist) Nikki Giovanni. Still, we all instinctively understood the black-power philosophy that had taken hold. People were standing up for themselves, no longer waiting for white folks to give us a piece of the American pie.

The band's playing is fiery, and their restraint masterful, while the bridge is augmented by horns, adding to the song's growing aura. Beal again plays some scorching guitar licks, here reminiscent of The Isley Brothers' Ernie Isley. The song fades out as we hear more off-the-cuff fooling around and talking, bringing side one to a close.

'C'mon Children (M. White, V. White, Beale, Whitehead, Flemons)
The album's writing trio to this point, are joined by Verdine and Beal, on a workout for their rhythmic chops. The pair's added input is immediately evident during the intro's fuzz guitar riff, before Verdine takes off with a complex bass groove. Maurice's vocal is mixed up-front in the verse, though we hear the other vocalists as they extol us to 'Come on down and lend a hand'. The verse's one-chord vamp is continued into the almost psychedelic B section, where trippy reverb and percussion are interrupted by the intro riff, launching straight into verse two.

Opening side two with the album's most unmemorable moment yet, the lack of a true hook holds the song back, but the individual players coming to the fore is a treat.

'This World Today' (White, Flemons, Whitehead)
After a brief but soulful introduction, the band snaps into a double time, continuously emphasised by a quick snare roll from Maurice. Verdine plays a pumping off-beat bass line as the horns swell behind the vocals.

The lyric tells the story of a world trying to find its way to love, with 'man fighting man' for 'no reason at all'. By the end, we're told that 'love, peace of mind, should be our thing'. The vocal and horn hooks set the track apart from the one before, and though it's not a standout, it moves along nicely and can easily get stuck in your head.

'Bad Tune' (M. White, V. White, Beal, Whitehead, Flemons)
The album's closer is an up-tempo romp, opening with thunder and lightning. This gives way to what may have been an unfamiliar sound for listeners in 1971: the kalimba. It's a traditional Central-and-Southern-African instrument, and a descendent of the m'bira, which was originally found in Zimbabwe. Both instruments and others in their family are often referred to as thumb pianos. The instrument has metal keys of different lengths that produce tones when played with the thumbs. These are attached to a wooden body which – like an acoustic guitar – can have a pickup installed to become electrified. The kalimba Maurice plays here is certainly bristling with electricity, and is most likely a distillation of the solos Ramsey Lewis used to encourage him to play during their shows. Gradually descending into a whirlwind of reverb and delay, the kalimba is soon interrupted by an energetic and hypnotic rhythm before more note flourishes. The instrument soon became highly associated with EW&F, and Maurice hoped he could use it to bridge the past and future in his own music.

Verdine's playing here is tight and clipped. Beal plays up a rhythmic storm as the horn lines fly past and accentuate the percussive shake. That's until the band stops the groove with a burst of Beal's fuzz guitar, which soon transforms into clean chords while he plays solo for a while. The band soon returns with a slow stomp, while the horns send a new melody into the air. Again the groove is changed to something more up-tempo as – with a sliding bass note – Verdine announces loudly that his fuzz pedal has arrived. But as soon as the groove hits its dynamic peak, the original rhythm is back, and so is the kalimba – floating from the speakers as the album draws to a close. The album left no doubt that the band's future was to hold something special, though perhaps no one predicted just how much success the group would have.

The Need of Love (1971)

Personnel:
Maurice White: vocals, drums, percussion, kalimba
Verdine White: bass
Don Whitehead: vocals, piano, electric piano
Yackov Ben Israel: percussion
Michael Beal: guitar, harmonica
Sherry Scott, Wade Flemons: vocals
Chet Washington: tenor saxophone
Alex Thomas: trombone
Leslie Drayton: trumpet
Oscar Brashear: trumpet
Producer: Joe Wissert
Engineer: Doug Botnick
Studio: Sunset Sound, Hollywood
Release date: November 1971
Chart positions: USA: 35 (Soul), UK: -
Running time: 31:47

The debut album sold a respectable 40,000 copies, prompting Warner Bros. to ask for a follow up. Before recording commenced, filmmaker Melvin Van Peebles offered for the group to play the score he'd written for his upcoming blaxploitation film *Sweet Sweetback's Baadasssss Song*. The film eventually became a classic (alongside *Coffy, Superfly* and the smash hit *Shaft*), giving black viewers a chance to see themselves as the hero, and reinforcing the genre's cultural relevance. Van Peebles helped pave the way for black, independent filmmakers while giving awareness to social issues – all on a shoestring budget.

Earth, Wind & Fire were hired cheaply to sketch out the music. (Maurice joked that Van Peebles' cheque was still bouncing 30 years later.) According to Maurice: 'He projected clips from the film he'd already shot, onto a wall in the studio. The engineer pressed record, and we played along to those clips. The images were violent, sexual and dark depictions of black life. Over two days, we recorded the entire score'. The end result was important for the group, helping them reach a new audience. Van Peebles had managed to get the soundtrack released on the legendary Stax label – an advantage that wasn't lost on Maurice. But however important the movie or its impact on the group, the album isn't one of their best efforts, and is probably best heard in the context of the film. Being a mishmash of film sounds and dialogue, EW&F playing frantic up-tempo funk, and Van Peebles doing some singing, the soundtrack is one for completists. And since no group members were involved in the writing process, it will be given no further investigation here.

With all this going on, the group was still planning to record their second LP, which was nearly derailed when Verdine's Vietnam war draft ticket came up. He avoided eating for roughly a month, and was – thankfully – given a deferment.

While touring to support their debut, the group had written five new pieces that brought their jazz influences and New Age philosophies to the fore. The album was again produced by Joe Wissert at Sunset Sound.

'Energy' (Scott, Whitehead, Flemons, White)

Of all the things that might open an EW&F album, a drum solo might be one of the most unexpected. Here, Maurice gives a glimpse into his concert solos as part of the Ramsey Lewis band. His prowess on the kit is too often ignored, and this fiery opening introduces the jazz-fusion-inspired opening track. Chet Washington takes a free-flowing and conversational solo as Maurice thunders along underneath – each of the two pushing the other to new levels of intensity. Out of the blue, this gives way to a solitary finger cymbal, and we're in a new musical environment with *Bitches Brew*-style trumpet and Sherry Scott talking us through what sounds like guided meditation. Scott's voice moves through the musical dynamics while the band indulges in a feedback-soaked exercise in free jazz.

Two minutes in, Maurice introduces a groovy drum rhythm, soon joined by keys, guitar, Verdine's booming bass, and completed by a catchy descending horn line. The lyric continues the vibe of the first album. 'Love is what we've got/Lets live it every day' is the driving message, until the music is broken up with silence, each vocalist taking a turn with their own phrase. The verse lyric flips the idea, alerting us to 'lots of people dying', with the dire statement that there 'ain't no love at all'. This is tempered by the message that if you 'give love from the heart/You'll always have a friend'. The group then fall again into a cacophony of blasting drum fills, roaring horns and wah guitar.

The free-jazz section is a one-chord groove that again seems inspired by *Bitches Brew*. Verdine's bass parts see him applying fast vibrato, and Beal again showcases his powerful rhythm guitar playing. Session trumpeter Oscar Brashear (uncredited in the liner notes) lays down a wild jazz-fusion solo for well over a minute, until the band again descends briefly into chaos. Maurice must have been impressed with Brashear's efforts because he became central to the EW&F horn sound on upcoming efforts. To say it's adventurous for an up-and-coming group to begin the follow-up to a reasonably successful debut with a ten-minute fusion and free-jazz workout is an understatement. This could've only occurred at that particular point in history – when acts like Weather Report and Mahavishnu Orchestra were taking jazz fusion into arenas.

'Beauty' (Flemons, White, Whitehead)

'Beauty' opens with Beal's shimming guitar, gently picking a suspended chord that rises and falls. A snare drum fill opens the door for Maurice and Verdine to lock into a tight groove (though nowhere near as tight as EW&F would later become). Verdine soon slides up his bass neck before landing on his intended note and shaking it violently – his soon-to-be signature glissando style, and the horns float above in a moment of R&B bliss. Flemons crooning gives the verse a smooth feeling, interrupted by a burst of horns that usher in a chord change over the same groove. The track drifts along nicely until the chorus, which is of particular note for being the first time EW&F used multiple ascending key changes in the one musical section. This eventually falls back to the first chord of the verse, and then repeats.

'I Can Feel It In My Bones' (Flemons, White, Whitehead)
This opens with a more-muscular riff than we've yet heard from EW&F – Beal's guitar souped-up with fuzz, and sounding not unlike Parliament/ Funkadelic (known as P-Funk) guitar extraordinaire Eddie Hazel. In fact, a lot about this track brings P-Funk to mind. Between the heavy riffing, Beal reminds us he's proficient on multiple instruments, blowing some bluesy harmonica. After the introduction, the horns and guitar lock into another rock riff, with gospel- style organ panned to the right. Maurice and Flemons start the verse, looking to a positive future, with the words 'I can feel it in my bones/Love is just around the corner'. A second fuzzed-out guitar closely follows the vocal melody – a technique used often by Jimi Hendrix and, indeed, P-Funk. The next section features saxophone flourishes and 'la la la' vocal harmonies. Sherry Scott's voice, in particular, sounds great sitting above the male vocalists. The track's second half is a mirror of the first and ends on a fade-out.

'I Think About Lovin' You' (Scott)
Finally, we come to a sung vocal from Sherry Scott, and her first solo writing credit on an EW&F album. She certainly makes the most of the opportunity to put her vocals front and centre, and sounds excellent while doing so.

It's a soul ballad, and after the piano intro, there are great vocal harmonies until Scott takes over. The chorus gives way to a great Motown-style verse, the melody of which recalls The Jackson Five's work of the era. Descending chords provide the bed until it's back to the chorus, in a more-powerful incarnation this time around. Don Whitehead's organ-playing fills out the sound, and Verdine and Maurice play their tightest groove so far.

A fade-out closes what might just be the album's finest track. Scott's songwriting talents come to the fore here, while the piece also works as a great vocal showcase.

'Everything Is Everything' (Powell, Church, Evans)
The longest piece here closes the album after only five tracks. It's a cover (rare for EW&F) of Donny Hathaway's 'Voices Inside (Everything Is Everything)'. Whitehead's blazing organ playing opens it, eventually joined by an electric-piano motif and clean guitar. The drums explode at around the

Earth, Wind and Fire ... On Track

two-minute mark, where Beal's fuzz guitar gives some rock power. Settling into the song's groove, it now becomes recognisable as the Donny Hathaway song. Hathaway's original feels a bit lighter and finishes at around three and a half minutes, while on this garage-funk take, EW&F are content to jam through to the end, varying musical elements and vamping on the chorus, while Beal sends some electric soloing into the ether. As the fade-out begins, it drops back to percussion and horns, which sounds great and would've been nice to hear more of.

This album doesn't necessarily see any improvement in songwriting from the first, but shows the group broadening its scope to fusion, free jazz and hard rock.

16

Last Days and Time (1972)

Personnel:
Maurice White: vocals, drums, kalimba
Verdine White: bass, vocals, percussion
Ralph Johnson: drums, percussion
Philip Bailey: vocals, congas, percussion
Roland Bautista: guitar, acoustic guitar
Larry Dunn: piano, organ, clavinet
Jessica Cleaves: vocals
Ronald Laws: soprano and tenor saxophone, flute
Oscar Brashear: trumpet
Producer: Joseph Wissert
Engineer: Al Schmitt
Studio: Sunset Sound, Hollywood
Release date: 1 November 1972
Chart positions: US: 87, US Soul: 15, UK: -
Running time: 39:52

The year between *The Need of Love* and *Last Days and Time* began as rocky for the group, though it proved to be essential to their existence and future success. *The Need of Love* sold roughly the same amount as the debut, which didn't sit well with some of the group or Warner Bros.. The blame was pointed at Maurice. Whitehead, Israel, Scott, Beal, Flemons and some of the horn section all left at the same time, leaving Maurice and Verdine to pick up the pieces.

The 28-year-old Maurice made it an imperative to hire younger, hungry musicians that he could mould to his own specifications, exceptional players who were also spiritually enlightened. Michael Beal put the brothers in contact with former Master's Children drummer Ralph Johnson, who was to share drumming duties with Maurice on recordings. Next came guitarist Roland Bautista, who blended funky rhythm-playing with hard rock licks and immediately clicked with Verdine's energetic personality. One Warner Bros. executive assigned to oversee the group, recommended two musicians who'd recently relocated from Denver, Colorado – 22-year-old vocalist/conga player Philip Bailey and 19-year-old keyboard wizard Larry Dunn.

At the time, working as musical director for Warner Bros. act The Stovell Sisters, Philip Bailey was nothing short of a revelation for the group. His percussive ability was certainly impressive, but his voice threatened to overshadow everything in its path. Bailey played drums as a child, and soon began singing. Early influences included Miles Davis and Stevie Wonder, and singers Sarah Vaughan and Dionne Warwick, whose styles, in particular, shaped his sound. Philip immediately hit it off with Maurice, and the pair were to become a formidable duo, understanding each other on a musical and conceptual level. In his autobiography *Shining Star*, Philip recalled conversations with Maurice about the band's goals: 'Earth, Wind & Fire's

17

premier mission has been to raise people to a higher level of consciousness. Maurice White called it 'The concept'. He'd sit me down and we'd talk about it for hours. He stressed the importance of the concept. He had drawings, charts and schematics of the band, detailing the concept'.

Bailey also rallied for Larry Dunn, contributing to the noise in Maurice's ear about the young keyboardist. Bailey convinced Maurice to audition his friend, and a run-through of a few EW&F songs and Herbie Hancock's 'Maiden Voyage' convinced all of Dunn's talent. Having started playing clubs at the age of 11, Dunn was ready for the spotlight, as he later the Schmooze Jazz website: 'I was playing jazz at a young age, and the group that Philip and I were in, and Andrew, we played everything from The Beatles to Jimmy Smith to The Temptations, The Supremes, every type of music – The Rolling Stones. So, you know, back in the day, to be in the band, there was one prerequisite: you had to play your instrument'.

A jazz-musician friend recommended saxophonist Ronald Laws, who was developing a name for himself as a smoking player. He soon became Maurice's favourite soloist in the band, routinely impressing with his jazz chops. Singer Helena Dixon completed the lineup, and the group worked up some new material. Opening live shows by sitting in yoga positions, they also openly incorporated their beliefs into performances.

Changes were also afoot behind the scenes, with talk of Warner Bros. wanting to drop EW&F. Taking this as a sign to reinvigorate the group, Maurice hired old friend Bob Cavallo as group manager, on the condition that he successfully navigate them out of their Warner Bros. contract. Cavallo responded by going full-throttle with the group's spiritual philosophy and new members, to help sell the act – eventually getting the group a showcase for music-industry mogul Clive Davis at Columbia Records. One 45-minute set later, and history was made. EW&F and Columbia were to have an incredibly successful run.

The pieces were all in place for the recording of *Last Days and Time*, only slightly derailed by one final lineup change, as Helena Dixon was replaced by the already successful Jessica Cleaves. Cleaves was a member of pop group The Friends of Distinction (who'd scored a smash hit with 'Grazing In The Grass'), and was known as an excellent vocalist. Trumpet players Bobby Bryant and Oscar Brashear were also hired. The group entered Sunset Sound Recorders with producer Joe Wissert again at the helm, though Maurice was beginning to have more production input. Famed artist Abdul Mati Klarwein – whose work includes the covers of Miles Davis' *Bitches Brew* and Santana's *Abraxas* – provided colourful and vibrant artwork, reinforcing the album's title's theme.

'Time Is On Your Side' (White, White, Bautista)

The album opens with a stomping funk blast. Not only has the playing improved, but the production is stronger and clearer. The horn section of Bryant, Brashear and Laws comes crashing out with the bass and drums after the very-first downbeat. The group settles into a steady vamp, Verdine supplying a nimble riff that outlines the chord. Bautista's time to prove his worth comes quickly as he blasts through the guitar offbeats, occasionally throwing wild flourishes into the percussive flurry.

Rather than giving away the talents of newcomers Cleaves and Bailey too soon, Maurice sings the first verse, afterwards joined by their full, gospel-like sound. A call-and-response unfolds, with Maurice demonstrating some newfound vocal chops. We get our first taste of Bailey's voice, hanging high above Maurice. The lyric provides a feeling of belonging and finding family:

Time is on your side
No more need in runnin', yeah
No more need to hide
No more need to cry, yeah

Maurice's lines 'Life is what you find, wanderin' in the sky' is almost surely a reference to astrology, and as time goes on, we'll see him further incorporate the subject into the band's music (let's not forget the group is named for his elemental symbols). The lyrics give off a positive vibe, and see the band looking ahead to what they were correctly convinced would be a bright future. They back this up by playing as if their lives depended on it, and a mid-song return to the intro sees them really cross into rock territory. The production reflects this by essentially capturing the group's live sound at the time, with an added sheen making them sound bigger and better than before.

'Interlude, No. 1' (White, White, Deason)

This is the first of three album interludes. Interestingly, the original US pressing doesn't list these amongst the track list, while certain, later foreign editions did – along with streaming platforms. The track is a brief 24-second burst of Ornette Coleman-esque saxophone. Sheets of dissonant sound rain down, jolting the listener. The sax eventually dies to a whimper. Though it's played by Ronald Laws, this and the other interludes credit the writers as being the White brothers and Sean Deason. In fact, these are the only credits listed to Deason's entire career – a strange mystery arising from the briefest of tracks.

'They Don't See' (Davis)

This song continues the album's uptempo trend, and was written by R&B master Mark Davis, who'd worked at Motown around the same time as Maurice, and produced albums for artists like Marvin Gaye and Diana Ross. The track is reasonably standard pop fare for the era, and at times sounds like a typical theme to a 1970s sitcom.

Bautista's guitar solo is a track highlight, and he's really given room to move here. His thick, woody tone recalls that employed by Denny Dias on early Steely Dan albums. Certain notes come in a machine-gun-like staccato, before settling into a simple melody. A lush bed of strings provides the padding, while the band provides a rock-steady foundation – Verdines playing in particular, seeming more calm than usual.

The lyric tackles the narrator's sadness about people who have lost their religious faith – which at times comes across as a little preachy. But the outro resounds with a universal theme, urging the listener to 'Love with all your heart'. Maurice really steps into more-soulful shoes here, and Bailey's vocal really stands out. The track closes with breathy group vocals, Cleaves being the loudest in the mix.

'Interlude, No. 2' (White, White, Deason)

While the first interlude could be interpreted as the group further exploring the jazz influences that came to the fore on the album before, this second interlude can only be described as a quick, whimsical break. Consisting of a quick piano ditty in the style of jazz icon Thelonious Monk, the track comes in at an extremely brief 23 seconds, with the sound of laughter filling the air after a humorous ending.

'Make It With You' (Gates)

This was a cover of Bread's smash hit from 1970. Following the original closely, the big change is, of course, the electrified, funky EW&F sound. It's also faster, and the percussion and keys come to the fore. Most notably, it has Philip Bailey's first full lead vocal, which comes across as a revelation – Bailey leans into his jazz tone and claims the song as his own.

'Power' (White)

Written by Maurice, this side-one closer is the purest distillation of his album vision, and it became an essential part of the group's early live shows. It begins with relaxing kalimba, before Bautista plays a groovy funk riff. Dunn plays some nasty clavinet, and Maurice takes a solo for a while, just as he did live, until Johnson kicks in with a big backbeat.

Verdine's bass riff doesn't disappoint, and Laws again proves his worth with a fine soprano sax solo. The band breaks away as Bautista fearlessly leads them towards a new riff, this time upping the funk factor with his wah pedal, and playing off Verdine's sparse bass line. When Bautista's solo comes, he begins rather tentatively, slowly building towards full-on fuzz mayhem, recalling P-Funk's Eddie Hazel.

An absolute powerhouse funk workout, 'Power' is EW&Fs first true instrumental journey. The group opened the next tour with it, and it's arguably their first truly essential track, despite having no vocals. Though not yet at the peak of their powers, they demonstrated that they were equal to the top funk and fusion acts of the day. Philip Bailey later said in *Shining Star*: 'From a purely stylistic standpoint, Earth, Wind & Fire was a commercial fusion group, as opposed to a funk band like Cameo or The Ohio Players'.

'Remember The Children' (White, White, Bautista)

After accents with horn stabs, we're pulled into a stomping groove with a minor-key riff from Bautista and Verdine. Dunn slides in slyly with his funk clavinet, and Bailey and Cleaves lock-in while they croon the backing vocal 'Remember children', and Maurice exhibits some vocal licks.Bailey takes over halfway through, upping the ante incredibly. As the horns add intensity, it sounds like it might fall apart in a discordant train wreck, until Bautista and Verdine save the day with their pumping chorus riff. The verse two lines 'See the message in their faces/Tell us what the future brings/Findin' far off places' are an example of the album's anti-war theme.

'Interlude, No. 3' (White, White, Deason)

This third interlude seems to have no ties whatsoever to the first and second, and would sound more at home in a 1970s Christmas drama film. A beautiful horn arrangement moves above the sound of children playing, but the music's drama suggests all is not right, and it ends on an unresolved chord. Certainly a more powerful and moving statement, it's so different to the other interludes and works better as an introduction to the next track.

'Where Have All The Flowers Gone' (Seeger)

This cover of Pete Seeger's folk classic puts the song in 6/8 and gives it a Motown-style makeover. Seeger's intention had been to talk about the cycles of war and the effects on those whose lives they touch. This theme fits with the album, though it was Clive Davis (rather than Maurice) who suggested the song.

Laid-back drums set the mood, and a melancholy horn line sounds in the distance. Dunn's organ swells fill the track with a broad musicality, Bailey brings another impressive performance, and cinematic strings under the chorus give another dimension. The bridge recalls Marvin Gaye's 'What's Going On', the percussion becomes more dominant, and there's a descending key change. Bailey lets loose on the last verse, hitting high notes with a rough intensity he'd later shy away from in favour of a smoother style. The outro shows his low register, proving he sounds just as good there. Overall it's a good, soulful take, but lacks the later EW&F polish.

'I'd Rather Have You' (Scarborough)

Something of a funk/R&B powerhouse, the prolific Skip Scarborough has written hits for Con Funk Shun, Patti LaBelle, Anita Baker, Valerie Carter, and Jessica Cleaves' old group The Friends of Distinction. Starting in a low register, Cleaves gradually ramps up her performance, the rhythm section arrives, and Maurice and Philip bring in backing vocals. The pair's voices were to become such a group signature that hearing them on their own is worth paying attention to here. But Cleaves is the one who really shines here, with Bautista and Verdine backing off the intensity until needed. The bridge is worth noting for containing the 'ba-ba' vocals that also were to later become one of the group's calling cards. The string and horn arrangement is a marvel – Maurice calling it in *My Life with Earth, Wind & Fire*, 'probably the most mature song EW&F had ever recorded up until that point'.

'Mom' (White, White)

Written as a tribute to the White's mother, the track brings the album to a close. At six minutes in length, 'Mom' suffers from the weight of its album sequencing but is strong enough to stand out. A bold string arrangement, grooving percussion and a soothing vocal help the verse take on a life of its own, unlike any other track on the album. The clave rhythm (and variants) is used in traditional Cuban music, such as mambo and salsa. Maurice steps up to the plate, delivering a soulful performance that's maybe his best up to this point.

The chorus horns strongly follow the clave rhythm, and the end section has a suspended chord that would be recalled later – particularly on the hit 'Fantasy'. Between the chorus and a fabulous Dunn solo, the strings are brought to new heights with a fast 16th-note passage in unison with a glockenspiel. 'Mom' shows the group painting on a much bigger canvas than before.

Head to the Sky (1973)

Personnel:
Maurice White: vocals, drums, kalimba, director
Verdine White: bass, vocals, percussion
Ralph Johnson: drums, percussion
Philip Bailey: vocals, congas, percussion
Al McKay: guitar, percussion, sitar
Johnny Graham: guitar, percussion
Larry Dunn: piano, organ, clavinet
Jessica Cleaves: vocals
Andrew Woolfolk: soprano saxophone, flute
Oscar Brashear: trumpet
Producer: Joseph Wissert
Engineer: Robert Appere
Studio: Sunset Sound, Hollywood
Mastering: Bernie Grundman
Release date: August 1973
Chart positions: US: 27, US R&B: 2, UK: -
Running time: 36:36

Head to the Sky is the sound of EW&F settling into their new sound and again lifting their game. Their 1970s story is one of a continued climb, and they were about to begin a steep ride to the top. First, there were more lineup changes to deal with – number one being Ronnie Laws, who left to join the band of famed South African trumpeter Hugh Masekela. Philip Bailey came to the rescue with an old friend from Colorado, Andrew Woolfolk. An incredible musician, his swift be-bop licks immediately fitting in.

Next to leave was Roland Bautista, citing financial issues. Maurice had already spotted guitarist Albert McKay. Born in New Orleans, McKay's family owned and lived above a bar and his bedroom was right above the stage. The music he heard coming up through the floor every night must've worked its way into him, and he became one of the all-time great funk guitarists. He realised early on that playing music was what he wanted to do, recalling to *Classic Pop* magazine:

I saw an Elvis movie called *Loving You*. It was in the third grade, but it affected me so much – the guitar, I just so loved it! I got one and never put it down. I played it upside-down for a year. I didn't know they made left-handed and right-handed guitars. What I'd got was a right-handed guitar, so, with no instructions, I learnt how to tune it to a straight E, and I kinda learnt how to play songs from there.

McKay performed and recorded with artists like Ike Turner, Sammy Davis Jr. and Isaac Hayes, and brought a wealth of experience to EW&F. But he had leftover commitments to attend to. Maurice was left scrambling for an emergency fill-in, but remembered young guitarist Johnny Graham, who'd developed a reputation as a blues soloist in the group New Birth. He was offered a role in EW&F as soon as he auditioned.

Once McKay joined the group, they headed back into the studio with producer Joe Wissert, though Maurice still considers his own production input on the album to be more important than Wissert's. *Head to the Sky* is where Maurice's vision began to fully crystallise, and the payoff was the top 50 hit 'Evil', which became a funk classic and a staple of their repertoire. It was as if the group's entire production had been supercharged, and *Head to the Sky* is the first classic album. *Rolling Stone* stated in their review: 'The vocals are breathy and soothing without being too ethereal. Altogether, they sound like a cosmic choir, and generate a Sly Stone effect. At its best, the music is fluid and enveloping, and most distinctive when Maurice White is playing an electrified kalimba (a small handheld African instrument) which produces delightfully-liquid runs of notes that have become the group's trademark'.

The group's image was also becoming more refined. The album cover – with all members bar Cleaves (who is seen wearing a white jumpsuit, which blends into the background) shirtless and surrounded by flowers – made it easy to see the group's intentions. In concert, the pea coats were ditched in favour of colourful outfits incorporating the group's African heritage, and in some ways predating the disco era. Maurice recalled in his autobiography: 'We were wearing more jewellery, and took on a more-ethnic vibe. We bought clothing at Capezio: a store that sold outfits for dancing. We mixed everything up: silk with leather; suede with paisley. It worked for us as long as it was cool in our own idiosyncratic eyes'.

Maurice also became more selective with which shows the band would play – no longer having to accept just anything that came along. The puzzle pieces were falling into place.

'Evil' (White, Bailey)

The album opens with a flash of furious thunder and lightning, and we are then greeted with jazz chord stabs trailed by lingering percussion that slowly fades away, creating a continuing motion like ocean waves. Dunn soon plays a Latin-jazz-inspired descending chord progression, at first backed only by a lone guiro – a ridged percussion instrument which is played by dragging a stick along its body. McKay and Graham immediately make a big difference with their locked-in groove. Verdine sits in the pocket while Maurice sends sparks of notes flying from the electric kalimba. The production is noticeably lusher. After a few rounds, Maurice begins a classic lead vocal. Bailey, Cleaves and Verdine sing backups to Maurice's pleas: sounding like an outer-space choir. Bailey's voice sits above in an ethereal falsetto draped in reverb.

The lyric deals with the idea of humankind having a sort of built-in evil, and how turning to love can save us all – brought to the fore in the opening lines 'Evil running through our brain/We and evil's about the same'. The entire album (and a good chunk of EW&F's music) was based on introspection and the awakening of spiritual consciousness, Maurice later saying, 'We wanted our audience to realise that to be young, gifted and black, it was necessary to be awake and sensitive to the inner, as well as the outer man'.

The bridge finds Bailey's vocal rising and falling, the melody conjuring images of spacecraft taking flight. Maurice brings back kalimba notes before beginning verse two. Maurice brings back his kalimba playing before beginning the second verse. The rock-solid rhythm section doesn't go unnoticed underneath all this. Following a return to the bridge, they jam on the groove until the end.

'Keep Your Head To The Sky' (White)

Written by Maurice – though he gave the lead vocal to Bailey – this track begins with chords that recall the opening of David Bowie's 'Fame' – both intros featuring guitar trills and hammer-ons recalling the guitar technique of soul master David T. Walker. A mid-tempo soul/pop groove is established as McKay plays a riff on an electric sitar. Bailey's soulfulness is evident from the first note. (He later re-recorded the song on his 2002 solo album *Soul on Jazz*.) Verdine also shines in the verse, and employs his high glissando style extremely effectively; the listener can hear Verdine's playing mature over the years, using this technique as a marker.

The smooth verse chords continue into the chorus, with lovely rhythm-playing from McKay and Graham. Heavenly backing vocals provide a sort-of call-and-response with Bailey's vocal runs, and eventually, chord changes are abandoned and it shifts to a one-chord vamp – the continuing undeterred. Bailey eventually joins in the backing vocals, answering his own pleas. At around 4:40, the music drops out, and there's one round of the vocal arrangement on its own. The lyric saw Maurice embracing his culture and applying his optimistic vision of the future, as he recalled in his autobiography: 'We wanted our black fans to stand tall and fulfil their highest potential from a position of cultural strength. My plan was to increase everybody's level of ethnic consciousness, forcing them to transcend into a philosophy that embraced all of humanity for the planet's highest good'.

'Build Your Nest' (M. White, V. White)

This might be the funkiest ode to making a home ever written. Dunn establishes a bopping double-clavinet riff over a quarter-note kick drum, until the entire band comes in with a hard 16ths groove. McKay holds down the chords while Graham lays down some tight lines. Organ fills out the verse, and vocals usher in a short section of descending chord stabs, before veering sharply into a new chord vamp where Bailey shows off his vocal chops. This is repeated, and it fades out at just over three minutes. Though certainly not an essential track, it's still a fun listen.

25

'The World's A Masquerade' (Scarborough)

The last track on side one is Skip Scarborough's second contribution EW&F – a soul ballad in 6/8 time. A strange, ringing, high synth note slowly descends in pitch. Verdine is locked into the pocket while McKay and Graham support from the back. Maurice is in full crooner mode as Dunn plays light chords.

Cleaves, Bailey and Verdine White, provide strong backing on the chorus, with Cleaves here standing out. The chorus provides an answer to the verse question, informing us that 'the whole world is a masquerade'. Emotive and well-played, the ballad never quite takes flight.

'Clover' (Dunn, White)

Larry Dunn talked about this track to smartalecmusic.com: 'That tune never ceases to amaze me, simply because of the way it happened. Maurice and I were in the studio, and I just started playing some chords. Then, the next thing you know, we had 'Clover''. Dunn's opening Fender Rhodes tremolo chords sound a lot like what became 1990s neo-soul.

Woolfolk's flute hovers around Maurice's vocal like a butterfly. A new segment with simple vocals leads to a snappy bridge key change, with Bailey and the backing vocals achieving an otherworldly quality as the flute continues to flutter by. Soon the music descends down, and a new section opens with a back-and-forth chord progression – Johnson's drums moving to double time. After its peak, Graham plays a thrilling Freddie King-style guitar solo, continuing as the track fades and Maurice is heard excitedly saying, 'Look like Johnny got it for ya'.

'Zanzibar' (Lobo)

A re-imagining of the piece by Brazilian bossa nova artist Edu Lobo, closes the album in style, the band presenting a 13-minute fusion workout. It's slower than Lobo's original version, the group is in no rush, and takes their time. It opens with the traditional Brazilian friction drum, the cuica (known as a monkey drum). Dunn provides chord padding as Johnson branches out. The entire group comes crashing in at around the two-minute mark.

Bailey, Maurice and Cleaves' scat singing drifts in and out of the chords and stabs. Verdine helps strengthen the album's bond with South American rhythms. Then comes a wonderful trumpet solo by Oscar Brashear, who continued to pop up – credited and uncredited – through EW&F's discography. The solo is smooth but firm, building momentum as it goes. Dunn's organ solo also satisfies with some scorching licks. Johnson soon arrives with some solid fuzz-guitar lines, followed up by a conga break from Philip Bailey. The group brings the dynamic down as Woolfolk's sax begins to cry out, eventually playing the notes with blistering speed.

Open Our Eyes (1974)

Personnel:
Maurice White: vocals, drums, kalimba
Verdine White: bass, vocals, percussion
Ralph Johnson, Fred White: drums, percussion
Philip Bailey: vocals, congas, percussion
Al McKay: guitar, percussion, vocals
Johnny Graham: guitar, percussion
Larry Dunn: piano, organ, Moog synthesizer
Andrew Woolfolk: soprano saxophone, flute
Oscar Brashear: trumpet
Producers: Joseph Wissert, Maurice White
Associate producer: Chris Stepney
Engineer: Bruce Botnick
Studio: Caribou Ranch, Nederland, Colorado
Mastering: Steve Hoffman
Release date: 25 March 1974
Chart positions: US: 15, 1 (R&B), UK: -
Running time: 39:51

With the group's confidence at an all-time high, they were shocked to hear that less than three weeks after the release of *Head to the Sky*, Columbia Records president Clive Davis – the group's biggest champion there – was fired due to misappropriation of funds (with plenty of rumours swirling around). Fearing they might lose their backing, the group was relieved when new president Walter Yetnikoff became a strong champion of EW&F, though it would take a long time for the dust to settle.

Before they recorded the next album, Jessica Cleaves left to move to Kansas. But this isn't the end of her story, as she later became a core member of George Clinton's Parliament/Funkadelic side project The Brides of Funkenstein.

Maurice continued to take the reins, acting as co-producer next to the dependable Joe Wissert. Looking to keep the band moving forward, Maurice brought in old Chess Records friend Chris Stepney, who'd been an arranger on albums by the Ramsey Lewis Trio. Maurice loved working with Stepney, and had always vowed to bring him into the fold once it was financially possible to do so. Larry Dunn told Red Bull Music Academy: 'When Chris Stepney put his thing on with the horns and the strings, it was like 'Wow'. I learned so many things about production from Maurice, but Charles being a keyboard player and arranger, meant a great deal. He was really in my corner'. Stepney brought in subtle changes, like keeping chord voicings out of the way of the vocals. Philip Bailey recalled in his autobiography *Shining Star*: 'Maurice and Charles had fire and swagger – they were a dynamic team. It was plain to see that the new songs on *Open Our Eyes* that featured

Stepney as engineer, arranger and producer, were getting tighter and tighter. Charles was leading us toward scoring that elusive hit record!'.

Joining the ranks was third White brother and drummer extraordinaire, Fred. Having cut his teeth touring with Donny Hathaway, and appearing on his hit *Live* album, Fred White was earning a considerable reputation as a hot player. He joined Lowell George's Little Feat – appearing on their album *Feats Don't Fail Me Now* – before Maurice and Verdine invited him aboard. From this point forward, Maurice and Fred handled the bulk of the studio drumming.

This time the group recorded at Caribou Ranch in the Rocky Mountains near Colorado. Built by James Guercio a few years earlier – and located over 8000 feet above sea level – the studio had already been used by acts like Joe Walsh, Chicago and The Beach Boys. Specifically picked to avoid the distractions of Los Angeles, Caribou worked its magic as the group improved its production, achieving their biggest album and single thus far.

Open Our Eyes opened the door to stardom a little further; the hard work was starting to pay off. The album yielded three charting singles – 'Mighty, Mighty' (29), 'Devotion' (33) and 'Kalimba Story' (55). *Open Our Eyes* is the last snapshot of EW&F before they truly arrived as one of pop's heavy hitters.

'Mighty Mighty' (White, White)
This is a blast of tight 1970s funk. The production is again improved, and the listener has to wonder how involved Joseph Wissart really was anymore, as the album bears little sonic resemblance to the first few. Maurice's vision was playing out in the form of Charles Stepney's production and engineering know-how. With the group tighter than before, their touring had clearly made an impact.

The massive rhythm-section groove laid the ground for the rest of the group. The pocket is much more developed than on *Head to the Sky*, and the tighter the group got, the more they were equipped with the sound required to be commercially successful. Fred White's debut is impressive, as he holds the groove down with authority. Dunn, Graham and the horns sketch out a complicated line while McKay grooves hard on a 16ths rhythm. Bailey – panned to the left – sounds even more confident and capable than before: his vocal performance astonishing.

But the chorus is the real selling point here. It's impossibly catchy and in a funky syncopated rhythm, tailed off with harmony scat vocals. The band here is on fire. The track's second half is a mirror image of the first, and by the time the second chorus rolls around, the hook is well stuck in the listener's head. Bailey's efforts are monumental. Maurice said of the song in his autobiography: 'Our message of empowerment urged our audience to seek education and embrace solid values. The message was for everyone, especially African Americans. I couldn't ignore racism. It was everywhere, from street corners to boardrooms'.

'Mighty Mighty' became a staple of the group's live repertoire for the rest of their career, and was heard on radio stations across America on its way to becoming a hit.

'Devotion' (White, Bailey)
'Devotion' is a soaring soul/funk ballad and a showcase for Bailey. A slow, funky groove is the foundation. Dunn plays a silky synth line over the intro. Verdine's bass shines as he stays in the pocket, also sneaking in some extra tricks to really set off the low end. Bailey takes the lead among the gospel vocals. When it reaches a peak, Verdine lays down an impressive run to send the group back to the chorus – during which Bailey really pulls the switch and lets loose an incredible falsetto yelp. The song form is similar to 'Mighty Mighty' in that it mirrors the first half, but being so strong, this doesn't detract at all. In concert, the group stretched-out sections to involve crowd participation and improvisation from Bailey.

Though written by Maurice and Phillip, Charles Stepney's fingerprints are all over the song, adding an extra level of chordal sophistication. In his autobiography, Philip Bailey remembers Stepney's work: 'When I first heard the finished version of 'Devotion', I was so impressed with the synths and chord changes that Stepney had added, that I concluded that the song wouldn't be effective without them'.

'Devotion' reached 23 in the US – the album's most successful single and the group's biggest hit to that point.

'Fair But So Uncool' (Stepney, Giles)
Stepney's first song on the album was co-written with Rick Giles, who later became a top country songwriter for artists like Reba McEntire, Tim McGraw and George Strait. The song breezes on a relaxed rhythm and Verdine's popping bass. It's the album's first track where Maurice plays the drums, and also his first lead vocal, where he adds Louis Armstrong-like dirt to his voice when the mood takes him.

'Feelin' Blue' (Altman)
The album's most outright jazz moment so far, was written by former rock/folk/jazz group Fifth Avenue Band bassist Kenny Altman. After a brief, synth-driven intro, the song breaks into a classy groove. Bailey and White handle the verse, with Al and Verdine stepping in with brilliant harmonies on certain phrases. Dunn's synth solo is tasteful, developing ideas throughout.

'Kalimba Story' (White, White)
The bass supports the drum groove with rock-solid quarter notes, Graham and McKay play thick chords and syncopated single-note parts, including the slightly overdriven riff. Maurice's lead vocal is drenched in psychedelic phaser swirls.

Saw it in a store one day
Thought it might make me play
Future music all for you
See me through my hardest time

The chorus maintains the lyric simplicity with 'Kalimba, oh kalimba/Play me a tune' over the same groove as the verse. But a sudden key change offsets this, bringing a sudden sense of urgency. Maurice really starts playing the kalimba in his own classic style here and becomes the centrepiece.

'Drum Song' (Maurice White)

Almost a musical answer to 'Kalimba Story', 'Drum Song' opens side two with kalimba patterns like a musical kaleidoscope. A strong groove locks in, with percussion galore and a descending riff from Maurice. The bass line propels the track with extra licks to keep things interesting.

'Tee Nine Chee Bit' (White, Stepney, Bailey)

This is a slow funk with a comedic vocal. Verdine establishes a tight bass line, and as the group joins in, we hear two male characters talking, and one of them appears to be about to commit murder with a butcher knife. Before long, the voice moves from gruff talking to singing, and it's revealed to be Maurice, who sings in character throughout. The groove really gets under your skin, and the chorus deviates just enough from the bass riff to keep things interesting. 'Tee Nine Chee Bit' is not an album high point, but it achieves what it sets out to do.

'Spasmodic Movements' (Harris)

Written by jazz saxophonist Eddie Harris, this is straight-ahead jazz. Harris has the distinction of being the first jazz musician to have a certified gold record (for his version of the *Exodus* theme), and his 'Freedom Jazz Dance' was later popularised by Miles Davis.

Side two is the album's more experimental side, opening with whirling, reverb-soaked percussion that soon makes way for the freewheeling sax of Woolfolk, who's really in fine form. Larry and Verdine really shine here – Verdine propelling the music with his walking bass line. EW&F show their love of jazz here, and they could play it as well as any group at the time.

'Rabbit Seed' (White)

32 seconds in length, 'Rabbit Seed' is a brief transition. Featuring percussion and group vocals, it's a bridge leading to the next track.

'Caribou' (Stepney, Giles)

'Caribou' opens with the kind of wordless vocals that became an EW&F signature. Maurice plays a syncopated snare rhythm, while Verdine and Larry match the jilted rhythm with chord stabs. A high group scream sends the track in the direction of McKay and Graham's harmonised guitar parts, at times reminiscent of Shuggie Otis' 'Strawberry Letter 23'. This all gives way to a great solo from Graham, which drifts in and out of harmony sections in a dream-like manner. Another high group wail brings in the final vocal section, which briefly repeats until a slightly abrupt ending. Named after the studio, 'Caribou' sees the band add more new elements to their sound, and the album's experimental nature is again explored to great effect.

'Open Our Eyes' (Lumkins)

Church bells adorn the opening few seconds of the gospel-like title track. A slow, steady 12/8 paves the way, and Verdine locks in hard with brother Fred, while Maurice's lead vocal makes itself the point of attention. The lyric really leans on the aforementioned gospel, Maurice executing vocal runs with occasional backing-vocal responses. The track slowly builds in intensity, growing louder with every vocal lick. Dunn's piano is overdubbed with synth in spots. Though it sounds a bit out of place, it gives the old-time feel a much-needed futuristic edge. Maurice really claims the song for himself, his performance is completely committed.

That's the Way of the World (1975)

Personnel:
Maurice White: vocals, drums, kalimba
Verdine White: bass, vocals, percussion
Ralph Johnson, Fred White: drums, percussion
Philip Bailey: vocals, congas, percussion
Al McKay: guitar, percussion, vocals
Johnny Graham: guitar, percussion
Larry Dunn: piano, organ, Moog synthesizer
Andrew Woolfolk: soprano saxophone, flute
Oscar Brashear: trumpet
George Bohanon: trombone
Producers: Maurice White, Chris Stepney
Engineer: George Massenburg
Studios: Caribou Ranch, Colorado; Sunset Sound, Hollywood
Mastering: Kendun Recorders, California
Release date: 15 March 1975
Chart positions: US: 1, 1 (R&B), UK: -
Running time: 38:54

This is the album that turned Earth, Wind and Fire into a household name
in America. Arriving almost a year to the day after *Open Our Eyes,* the group
were back and bigger than ever. They worked hard between albums, and two
concerts, in particular, helped advance awareness of the group. The California
Jam was a nationally televised rock festival held in April 1974, and featured
some of the biggest rock acts of the time. While headline acts Deep Purple
and Emerson, Lake & Palmer attacked cameras and amplifiers and argued
about when they would play, groups from earlier in the day like EW&F and
Eagles (with guest Jackson Browne) made a lasting musical impression on
the audience. Later in 1974, EW&F opened for Sly and The Family Stone at
New York's prestigious Madison Square Garden arena. Maurice remembered:
'Verdine had acquired the actual harness that Mary Martin used in *Peter Pan*.
At the appointed moment, he shot straight up in the air like a rocket and
hung high above the stage; his legs wildly flailing in the air while he kept on
playing his Fender bass. The Garden went into a full-on frenzy'.

During this time, Maurice reunited with Ramsey Lewis, who hired EW&F
for his 1974 album *Sun Goddess*. The album became a major hit with the jazz
fusion crowd, climbing to number 1 on the Jazz chart and 12 on the Billboard
200 – further helping to cement EW&F's glowing reputation with lovers of
great playing.

Maurice was already plotting the next move – a concept album based on
the biblical story of the Tower of Babel – when he got a call from filmmaker
Sig Shore. Shore was coming off the back of his hit film *Superfly,* and needed
a group to not only provide the soundtrack to his new project *That's the Way*

of the World, but also act in it. The movie was to star Hollywood leading man Harvey Keitel. Curtis Mayfield's soundtrack to *Superfly* had proved to be a bigger success than the movie itself: a positive sign for EW&F. The resulting album's artwork would also be separate from the movie, providing another buffer against failure. Despite some concerns, Maurice accepted the offer, also benefitting from an increased recording budget.

The film itself began with footage of the group playing the title track in the studio, with live concert footage of the group scattered throughout. It's great to see EW&F like this, despite Maurice' saying the group looked like 'clowns' after he and Verdine went to a test screening. Keitel plays record producer Coleman Buckmaster, who is working on the first album by The Group. But instead, he's forced to produce fictional act Pages (not the late-1970s West Coast group), who – according to the label head – project a more-wholesome image than The Group. Spoiler ahead – through numerous dramatic plot twists, Buckmaster manages to reunite with The Group, and all is well by the end. With EW&F billed just below Keitel on movie posters and using all original music, *That's the Way of the World* turned out to be a great move. Though the movie itself bombed, EW&F had hit the big time.

The group were expanding, with Maurice finally getting a sole producer credit. Chris Stepney – so instrumental in the making of *Open Our Eyes* – returned as co-producer. Verdine recalled making the album to mixonline. com: 'This was an important album – one that signalled whether we would go on and become a mainstream group, or just be an R&B act. At that particular time – which is different than radio today – they didn't really cross a lot of black acts over to mainstream radio. We already had two gold albums, but still, most of the mainstream didn't know who we were'.

The mainstream found out soon enough – the album hit number 1, and 'Shining Star' became a number-1 single, making EW&F the first black group to top both charts. 'Shining Star' also earned them a Grammy for Best R&B Performance by a Duo or Group. 1975 was truly Earth, Wind & Fire's year, and began their run of hits. Some consider this era to be the group's artistic peak. Verdine told *Billboard* in 2001: 'We were always talking about universality, but I think it probably happened with *That's the Way of the World*'.

'Shining Star' (White, Bailey, Dunn)

'Shining Star' eclipsed all the EW&F hits before it, and was the next logical step. Graham and McKay open with a funky, intertwined harmony riff, with just enough phaser to give a swirly, shimmering vibe. A blast from the renewed horn section brings in the full groove. Stepney expertly wrote the horn arrangement, which was recorded not at Caribou but at Sunset Sound.

The verses are split between Maurice and Philip, Maurice taking a rhythmically punchy approach, and Bailey sending it out to the stratosphere as usual. The memorable chorus passes unbelievably quickly the first time.

Maurice recalled to *Mixonline.com*: 'The verse is rockin' and the chorus is much smoother. That's what we were going for – the contrast between the chorus to the verse, so it would give you a lift. To make the choruses smoother, we would add more reverb and a different EQ.

The detailed production became one of the things EW&F would be known for, particularly Maurice, as he became a studio master. The chorus concludes with brief solos from Dunn and McKay, the horns acting as a hook for the section. Bailey's runs stand out in the mix, and his first notes in verse two show his mesmerising range.

The importance of 'Shining Star' in the group's catalogue cannot be overstated. Their first number one hit, it became a funk classic. It's a perfect mix of density and simplicity, and can be appreciated by audiophiles and dance-floor partygoers alike.

'That's The Way Of The World' (White, White, Stepney)

This track sparkles with self-assurance. The soundscape is larger and more cohesive than their previous attempts at the soul genre – in no small part thanks to Stepney's string arrangement. Dunn's gorgeous intro organ-playing is bolstered by sweet strings, and if you haven't heard the track before, you know you're in for something special. The thumping heartbeat of the kick drum keeps the groove alive. A tom fill pushes the group forward, Verdine and the guitarists sitting wonderfully in the pocket. The strings perfectly augment the horns' understated line.

The verse vocals occur over the same chords as the chorus; Maurice and Philip sitting just behind the beat, anticipating the 1990s neo-soul of D'Angelo (who later recorded an incredible cover of EW&F's 'Can't Hide Love' on his *Live at the Jazz Cafe*). The chorus hits just as hard on its second appearance, and the intro returns before Graham takes a bluesy Freddie King-style solo.

The nostalgia is matched by the lyric, encouraging the listener to always look for the light in the darkness. Dunn addressed the subject in a Red Bull Music Academy interview:

We were trying to create music with a message and a meaning. That's who we were. We were trying to bring some light into a very dark world. The great thing about the legacy of our music is it had something to say and it meant what it said. People could dance to it, cry to it, chill to it and do whatever you want to do to it. Underneath that beautiful music was some vernacular that was really saying something pertinent.

'Happy Feelin' (White, White, Bailey, Dunn, McKay)

More of a group effort, 'Happy Feelin' is smooth up-tempo funk. A busy drum groove is joined by joyous guitar and keys playing chords over a classic Verdine bass riff. The horns play a fast lick sounding something like fellow funksters Tower of Power. Soon Bailey lets loose with the hooky chorus.

The intro horn line returns, and Maurice provides the album's first taste of kalimba, which soon leads to slightly uncharacteristic guitar harmonies. Woolfolk lays down some fiery licks that open the door to the verse and the multiple Bailey unison overdubs. The song is Bailey's for the taking. One of the most memorable parts is Dunn's brief organ part – seemingly tacked onto the end and lasting for around 20 seconds.

'All About Love (First Impression)' (White, Dunn)

The album's second ballad doesn't quite rise to the heights of 'That's The Way Of The World', but it is still exceptional. Beginning with Maurice speaking over 12/8 piano chords and sticky sweet strings, the track occasionally borders on being schmaltzy, but the group pulls it off. A later big-band section may be the most grandiose piece of music EW&F had recorded to this point, and Stepney's arrangement is really a treat.

The next verse brings a second, longer spoken-word section. The orchestra rises and falls underneath, but the focus is on Maurice's preaching. Eventually, he bursts into a vocal solo, really showing how far his chops have come, before it ends with a fade-out.

This might not be the album's most talked-about song, but the production shines, and Stepney's arrangement is irresistible. Dunn's synth theme re-emerges post fade out, and begins a longer version of the outro from 'Happy Feelin', this time with an added B section.

'Yearnin' Learnin'' (White, Bailey, Stepney)

Side two begins with this absolute barnstormer. It's one of the group's hardest-hitting funk pieces and has remained a staple in their live set to this day. Dunn begins with a piano riff moving between two chords, followed by the group laying down a syncopated rhythm. The track features every member of the group on percussion, demonstrating the need to get the groove across. Maurice takes all the vocal tracks on his own, with excellent results – his lyric reminding everyone in the band not to forget about working hard and staying focused despite the success that's coming their way:

Stop, look behind you
Fame and love gonna find you
We're just here to remind you
Yearn and learn is what you do

With the monstrous chorus established right off the bat, the group swerves into the steady verse rhythm. Maurice executes his vocal part with expertise, particularly towards the end of the verse and the pre-chorus as he performs vocal runs that melt across the chord changes. The compelling music was written by Stepney, and McKay remembered his importance to the group when talking to *Vintage Guitar Magazine:* "Yearnin' Learnin'" was his music.

He did all our arrangements, and I especially remember those dates because I learned new chords. It was like school, and it was one of the best times of my life. I played a Gibson L-5 on 'Yearnin' Learnin'.' It was a great day, a great song, and we loved it right away'.

'Reasons' (White, Bailey, Stepney)

'Reasons' went on to become an R&B standard, featured in movies, pop culture, and became famous for its message, ironically being used at numerous weddings. Bailey told *Entertainment Weekly*: 'It's funny, 'cause people say, 'We played that song at my wedding', and I'm like, 'Did you listen to the lyrics?'. The song is talking about a one-night stand. Me and Maurice were talking about the on-the-road life; what was going on at that time. It's totally lust for the moment'.

After a brief introduction with a catchy horn line and Bailey vocal harmonies, the verse arrives, smooth, breezy and danceable. The bass grooves along as Bailey's silky vocals become the focal point for listeners, who at first may miss finer details like the tightness of the percussion and drums together. The vocal melody is stunning, and Stepney's orchestration builds the track into an epic.

Instead of a second chorus, we are taken to a bridge with a hook strong enough to act as a bonus chorus. The horns peak here, continuing the intensity into the third verse. Exuding a film-like quality, the score takes the listener away to a place where only this song exists.

This is one of the all-time great R&B tracks, and is even more ammunition for the argument that this album is EW&F's pinnacle.

'Africano' (White, Dunn)

The album's first instrumental opens with a Woolfolk flute solo, at first on its own, before another joins in on a descending lick, drifting over a bed of Maurice's kalimba and vocals. A rapid-fire timbale fill brings the group to life as they begin their funk odyssey.

The horn section takes a call-and-response section, engaging Verdine along the way. Then comes a hot Woolfolk sax solo. This is really his track. A new horn line is introduced, followed by rising and falling chord changes. The track feels like it could go for longer and keep the listener completely engaged.

'See The Light' (Anglin, Dunn, Bailey)

The final track sees the group bringing some jazz fusion to the party. Starting with a Dunn and Verdine riff in 7/8, Dunn's synth then brings a sci-fi vibe against the earthy percussion. Bailey's vocal line matches the timing as the horn section throws out spiralling fusion licks. 'Troubles everywhere/More than I can bear', Bailey sings, the chaotic band performance matching it. In the next section, he hits a high note like a banshee scream, Maurice then joining in harmony. The band and orchestra outline a series of rhythmic hits following the line 'Let them see the light', changing the rhythm to a straight 4/4 groove, and the dense fusion is replaced with a feeling of peace.

The jazz changes accompanying the line 'Help me see them see the light', bring a feeling of vastness, leading to a new vocal part following another Dunn solo. This continues to the fade out. We then hear a reprise of the Dunn synth theme heard at the end of side one. This time the strange chord movement is joined by percussion and vocals.

Gratitude (1975)

Personnel:
Maurice White: vocals, drums, kalimba, timbales
Verdine White: bass, vocals, percussion
Ralph Johnson, Fred White: drums, percussion
Philip Bailey: vocals, congas, percussion
Al McKay: guitar, percussion, vocals
Johnny Graham: guitar, percussion
Larry Dunn: piano, organ, Moog synthesizer
Andrew Woolfolk: soprano saxophone, flute
Louis Satterfield: trombone
Michael Harris: trumpet
Don Myrick: saxophone
Producers: Maurice White, Charles Stepney, Joe Wissert, Chris Stepney
Engineers: George Massenburg, Cameron Marcarelli
Live Engineer: Wally Heider
Studios: Hollywood Sound Recorders, Wally Heider Studios, California
Mastering: Steve Hall, Mark Wilder
Release date: 15 March 1975
Chart positions: US: 1, 1 (R&B), UK: -
Running time: 38:54

Gratitude was half live and half studio tracks. Multiple artists experimented with this format at the time, including Kiss and ZZ Top. The live tracks were recorded via a mobile recording truck by engineer Wally Heider. This chapter will only discuss the studio tracks, however, the live recordings are recommended as a testament to the group's stunning live power at the time. Maurice recalled in *My Life With Earth, Wind & Fire*: 'The success gave the band a new start. Long gone was the very personal sting of the first group leaving; long gone was the revolving door of getting the new and right guys. Hertz station wagons had become limos and custom buses. Holiday Inns had given way to four-star hotels'.

This album introduced the sound that partly defined the band for the rest of the decade: The Phenix Horns. After a performance on the popular TV show *Midnight Special*, Maurice felt that the sound was good but not as full as he wanted, so he turned to an old pal from Chicago – bassist Louis Satterfield, who'd been a Chess Records session player with Maurice, but was now playing trombone. He brought with him bandmates from his former act The Pharaohs – trumpet player Michael Harris (later to be joined by Rahmlee Michael Davis), and saxophonist Don Myrick. Woolfolk remained – on soprano sax – as a permanent group member, whereas The Phenix Horns were considered a separate entity for hire. The new horn section immediately stepped up the group's game, showing incredible power and a staccato style that was to become incredibly influential (think *Off The Wall*-era Michael Jackson).

Gratitude is remembered as a great live funk album, and the studio recorded side a success, hitting number one in the US for three weeks and spending six weeks at the top of the Soul chart. The single and studio track 'Sing A Song' reached number five, and 'Can't Hide Love' hit 11 on the soul chart and was nominated for a Grammy.

'Interlude, No. 1' (White)
After the album's rousing first two sides of live performance, we enter the studio portion, though the interlude (unlisted on the original vinyl version) was barely long enough to make much of a statement.

'Sunshine' (White, Bailey, McKay, Dunn)
An unusual, kaleidoscopic guitar and bass line opens 'Sunshine', twisting around its funky groove until the group comes in to stabilise it. The Phenix Horns are immediately recognisable with their tight and high parts, while the drums hold down a firm Bo Diddley-like beat. Gorgeous production with an incredibly crisp top end shows how far the group has come – the kick drum, in particular, having a sound that would come to dominate dance music.

In the chorus, it becomes apparent how the syncopated blasts of The Phenix Horns transformed the group, adding a more commercial edge, and often in counterpoint to the vocal parts.

'Sing A Song' (White, McKay)
'Sing A Song' drips with positive sentiment, and is among the group's finest moments. McKay starts with an Ernie Isley-style guitar lick. From there, he lays down some of his finest single-note funk. Legend has it that McKay wrote the part while backstage in the dressing room. The horn's 16th notes are jaw-dropping in their execution, and as tight as any horn parts before or since. Fred keeps the groove straight down the middle, while Verdine takes some liberties and plays around with the bass line. The production values are really at the cutting edge of pop music at this point – the group beginning to take aim at the burgeoning disco genre.

Maurice and Philip's multi-layered vocals unfold, and Dunn joins Verdine's bass with a squelchy, funky synth line that adds to the enormity of the chorus. The Phenix Horns answer Verdine's verse lines, and by the next chorus, they play amazing lines alongside the vocals.

When the chorus returns, an added refrain throws the listener off with what turns out to be a false ending. The vocals descend until interrupted by the familiar groove, McKay's guitar line going strong. The synth returns as the track fades out.

'Gratitude' (White, White, Dunn)
Here the groove slows down to a mid-tempo stomp. Opening with spiralling Dunn chords, the horns join in. The 'Wanna thank you' line keeps things

simple and memorable. Verdine thumps out the bass line, while The Phenix Horns demonstrate their dynamic range against the steady groove. Maurice's words revel in the music and its relation to his spiritual interests.

Freedom in your stride
Love and peace of mind
We just wanna give gratitude
Got plenty love we wanna give to you
Through good music, we're trying to say
That the good Lord's gonna make a way

We are eventually treated to a key change, keeping the audience engaged while retaining the groove. 'Gratitude' is down-tempo funk at its best, the group retaining their cool, smooth demeanour throughout.

'Celebrate' (White, Bailey, Stepney)
The tempo is picked up again for 'Celebrate', and after a brief intro sees the horns hammer out a melody, McKay plays a clipped, staccato part that would be funky even on its own. The studio tracks here are really where McKay's style crystallises, placing him in the pantheon of funk guitar greats, along with Prince, Nile Rogers, and others. The drum groove is noticeably all kick and hi-hats, with snare being spared for now.

Two descending horn notes bring in the chorus, and the snare breaks the hypnotic spell, bringing a pounding four-on-the-floor groove. The band pivots between two chords for the most part, the vocals becoming more rhythmic to match. The horns have some excellent answers for Maurice and Philip, while Verdine really lays it down. A quick key change and break for some sprightly horns is the signal to repeat this part of the track. The verse jazz chords return, as does the mesmerising groove, albeit not for long.

It's a track of interesting contrast, but always with purpose and never to the song's detriment. This kind of progressive mindset helped set EW&F apart from similar acts of the era, as did their jazz and fusion influences.

'Interlude, No. 2' (White)
The second interlude has barely anything in common with the first. A brief funk workout, it's good fun, though too brief to leave much of an impression.

'Can't Hide Love' (Scarborough)
This genuine classic closes *Gratitude* on a high note. It was originally recorded by American R&B group Creative Source in 1973. The EW&F arrangement is strikingly different, sounding more like something from their first two albums. The track became an essential part of their catalogue, and a testament to their creative powers. This was in no small part due to the wizardry of Charles Stepney, as Maurice recalled in *My Life With Earth, Wind*

& Fire: 'Step had known from the day I met him back in Chicago, that I was the biggest sucker for John Coltrane. All he had to say was that this was something Trane would do, and I'd be all over it. When he first played the quick whole-tone ascending chord movement in the 'Can't Hide Love' intro, he had me big-time'.

The first four climbing horn blasts might fool the listener into thinking a fast disco track is coming, but we soon find that's not the case. The group settles into a steady slow 16ths rhythm, punctuated in places by those opening notes. Minimal drums and bass set the stage for Maurice's crooning vocal. The lyric concerns an admirer unable to hide their feelings, a pretty simple premise that sometimes comes across as bitterness on the narrator's part.

The Phenix Horns join in the second half of the verse and ever-building pre-chorus. Bailey takes over for the chorus, soaring above the group while Maurice keeps the track grounded with his lower register. The chorus climaxes with Maurice crying out 'I can't hide' as Bailey responds from the heavens, 'Feel inside'. Verse two brings us back down smoothly, and after another round of each section, Maurice lets loose over the back-and-forth bridge progression. This soon transforms into a chanting vocal section, bringing a sense of mystery.

'Can't Hide Love' closes *Gratitude* in style, with a glimpse into the group's next direction.

Spirit (1976)

Personnel:
Maurice White: vocals, drums, kalimba, timbales
Verdine White: bass, vocals, percussion
Ralph Johnson, Fred White: drums, percussion
Philip Bailey: vocals, congas, percussion
Al McKay: guitar, percussion
Johnny Graham: guitar
Larry Dunn: piano, organ, Moog synthesizer
Andrew Woolfolk: soprano saxophone, winds, percussion
Louis Satterfield: trombone
Michael Harris, Oscar Brashear: trumpet
Don Myrick: saxophone
Additional Musicians:
Charles Loper, George Bohanon: trombone
Tommy Johnson: tuba
Steve Madaio, Chuck Findley: trumpet
Art Maebe, David Duke: french horn
Marilyn Robinson, Sidney Muldrow: french horn
Harvey Mason: percussion
Producers: Maurice White, Charles Stepney
Engineers: George Massenburg, Richard Goodman, Dean Rod
Studios: Hollywood Sound Recorders, Wally Heider Studios, Westlake Audio,
Burbank Studios, Los Angeles, California
Mastering: Mark Wilder
Release date: 28 September 1976
Chart positions: US: 2, US R&B: 2 , UK: -
Running time: 36:21

The group's success didn't halt Maurice's entrepreneurial spirit, as he and
Charles Stepney founded Kalimba Productions. Originally conceived as a
means to lease out Maurice's production talents, he would recall in *My Life
With Earth, Wind & Fire*: 'in those early days I ran Kalimba Productions like
a record company, signing artists, paying advances and issuing royalties. But
Kalimba wasn't a record company. What I had was a distribution deal with
CBS Records. Some of the funding came from CBS/Columbia, and some came
from my pocket'. Maurice could now use EW&F's success to help provide a
platform for other artist's music, and himself with a chance to produce other
acts. By mid-1976, he was working on Deniece William's debut *This is Niecy,*
Ramsey Lewis' *Salongo,* The Emotions' *Flowers,* and *Spirit* itself. To cope with
the workload, and maintain high quality, he surrounded himself with a team
of experts. Producers, songwriters and arrangers would all be kept under the
company's wing, and also Charles Stepney, Larry Dunn, Al McKay and Verdine
White. Even with all this going on, the quality of *Spirit* was not compromised. A

demo by two young songwriters (Bernard Taylor and Peter Cor) set the vibe for the entire album, so blown away were the group by the pair's song 'Getaway'.

But tragedy struck unexpectedly when Stepney suffered a heart attack in his Hollywood hotel. Having finished all but three of the album's arrangements, Stepney was confined to a hospital bed, unable to work. Maurice utilised Tom Washington and Jerry Peters for the remaining tracks. However, this wasn't the end of Stepney's troubles. Upon returning home, he suffered a fatal heart attack in his doorway – aged only 45. His death was a devastating blow to the group, for whom everything else was coming up roses. In only a few short years, Stepney had helped fast-track the group's progress, and taken their production and arrangements to places others could only dream of. *Spirit* was dedicated to Stepney, with the liner notes containing a eulogy to their fallen friend.

A fleet of extra horn players added to the lineup, making the album immense and powerful. This included four french horns, three extra trombones, three extra trumpets and a tuba, all on top of Woolfolk and The Phenix Horns. The artwork showed the band arranged in front of three pyramids of bright light – representing the album's spiritual ambition, and also being a tribute to Stepney. This tied in with the stage show, which saw the group climb to the next level of arena production with glowing onstage pyramids with hydraulic doors. By the end of the *Spirit* tour, EW&F were one of the most successful touring acts in America, out-grossing The Eagles and Elton John. Maurice remembered in *My Life With Earth, Wind & Fire*: 'On the opening night of the tour, the stage was filled with three massive pyramids surrounded by fog. The lights rose as the hydraulic doors slowly opened, revealing us standing there dressed in robes, silently glaring at the audience. I'd never heard anything like the roar of the crowd. It was an earthquake-like rumble that was deafening'.

'Getaway' (Taylor, Cor)

'Getaway' bursts out of the speakers, barely able to contain itself with a complex, bebop-inspired vocal and instrumental opening passage sounding not unlike Maurice's friend's Weather Report. The four-bar line is a beacon indicating the new direction of EW&F's uptempo pieces – the group never shying away from their jazz roots but always keeping them accessible for pop audiences. Written by up-and-coming songwriters Bernard 'Beloyd' Taylor and Peter Cor (who went on to score television, commercials and movies), the demo had been on a tape that Verdine handed to Maurice. Cor discussed the track with *Soulmusic.com*:

Ironically, while we were writing the tune, even before connecting with EW&F, we told each other that we could hear them doing it. The engineer on our demo lived in the same apartment building as Verdine and a couple other group members, played them the demo we made, and they created their arrangement from that. Also, their producer Charles Stepney passed away while they were working on our tune, which could not have helped them any, but they finished it, and three months later, it was on the radio everywhere.

Maurice was blown away by the demo, and EW&F's interpretation was a career high point for both writers. The percussion – played partly by drummer extraordinaire Harvey Mason – is crisp and tight. By the end of the intro, it settles into a racing groove with a syncopated horn line burning over the top. McKay's playing helps create an impossibly funky groove to move the track forward. The end of the horn line is joined by Maurice and Bailey's 'Getaway, let's leave today' hook prior to the verse. The bass part is perfect in its simplicity – avoiding complicating the arrangement. A brief instrumental break shows the stabbing, staccato horn style introduced on *Gratitude*, though here it's more fully developed.

Maurice begins the verse, seeming to offer a way out for a troubled acquaintance.

Try to resist all the hurt that's all around you
If you taste it, it will haunt you

In the pre-chorus, he offers the solution, 'So come, take me by the hand/ We'll leave this troubled land'. The group eventually take a left turn, the snare dropping out leaving a thumping kick and hi-hat, while Bailey leads the group in a melody that spirals upwards before exploding back into the chorus. In verse two, Bailey executes multi-tracked vocals like his life depends on it. The pre-chorus, this time, leads to another verse, after which we get the full section in all its spiralling glory. Following this, the chorus and its resulting groove are undeniable in their strength, and Bailey's 'Getaway, leave today/Getaway, yeah yeah yeah' hook really is the cherry on top.

'Getaway' became a fan favourite, reaching 12 on the singles chart, and number one on the soul chart.

'On Your Face' (White, Bailey, Stepney)
A mid-tempo groove and a back-and-forth chord progression are a great background for this positive message. Handclaps with the snare drum add to the positive vibe. The bass is well in the pocket, Verdine throwing out the occasional lick for good measure, while the guitar tumbles around nicely. Maurice said of the track in *My Life With Earth, Wind & Fire*: 'That mellow feeling was probably just a reflection of the cosmic vibe around us'.

The groove soon changes for the chorus and more-conventional chord changes.

Sadness bears no remedy for the problems in your life
While you run your race
Keep a smiling face
Help you set your pace

After further spicy vocals from Maurice and Philip, the group ride it out until the end.

'On Your Face' was a minor hit, reaching 26 on the Soul chart.

'Imagination' (Stepney)

Next comes Charles Stepney's gorgeous ballad. It's one of Bailey's finest vocal performances, in a romantic tale of longing – the group providing a churning, soulful backing. The arrangement is strongly cinematic; the mix broad and full of percussion subtleties. Verdine later described the track to Greg Prato of *Songfacts.com* as one of EW&F's most underrated recordings.

Beginning with the horns and strings climbing through the chords, the band holds steady until settling into a groove that heralds the arrival of the vocals. The chords sound sweet but slightly sinister before the first verse settles on soulful shores. A long chord sequence makes up the verse, Bailey working his way through with no problem at all. A twinkling glockenspiel accentuates the melody, adding to the overall sugary feel. The main vocals have an almost whispered, intimate quality, as Bailey responds with fiery licks.

The outro is really where Bailey takes his vocal to another level – rising to the occasion for Charles Stepney's final EW&F songwriting contribution.

'Spirit' (White, Dunn)

Dunn plays Fender Rhodes electric piano to open the title track, with chord changes that slightly recall Coltrane's 'Giant Steps'. The lyric voices the group's commitment to their spiritual beliefs, set to slow, jazz chord changes. A remarkably high Bailey note kicks the group into action – his voice sounding like a vocal from a lost 1940s jazz classic. A smoky vibe pervades the verse, and we are taken on a mountainous journey until a steady drum rhythm appears. Verdine locks in, keeping the music driving forward, until the groove disappears, eventually returning after more stacked vocals.

'Saturday Night' (White, Bailey, McKay)

Side two starts by giving the listener no choice but to dance – Maurice laying down the drum rhythm and counting the group in before a horn stab. The single was the group's first charting recording in the UK – reaching 17 – and also hitting 21 in the US.

The stuttering kick pattern and a cracking snare are augmented by tight percussion. The catchy horn line is topped by a higher harmony the second time around, before the guitar and synth take over for the main instrumental line. 'Saturday night, shining down' Maurice and Philip sing, while McKay begins another of his clucky single-note guitar lines, before Maurice takes the verse alone. The verse leads to Bailey's melodic nursery rhyme-like chorus. With mentions of London Bridge, and Humpty Dumpty falling down, this would seem like an intentional move from the group. The hooks build up, and eventually ease as McKay's punchy guitar becomes the focal point.

'Earth, Wind & Fire' (White, Scarborough)

This lyric is a vessel to communicate the group's spiritual philosophy. The symphonic arrangement is a wide, sweeping panorama of sound behind the group. Quick, ascending stabs herald the arrival of the groove, interrupted by more accents, with the vocals joining in. McKay's distinctive rhythm playing is heard with just enough chorus effect to contrast with the other tracks. It supports Maurice's sparse verse melody, while Bailey's backing vocals build the verse's second half, before the string section elevates the chorus further. The chorus lyric lays out the EW&F philosophy as bare as it can, and Maurice continues to detail it – the second verse saying, 'World goes by the hand of the master plan/Can't you understand, you're but a grain of sand'. Luckily the group is more than up to backing this testament – though, ironically, it may not be the first song one thinks of when the name Earth, Wind & Fire is mentioned.

'Departure' (White, Dunn)

A brief, relaxing interlude, 'Departure' is 27 seconds long, and – true to its title – sounds much like the music heard in airport departure lounges around the world.

'Biyo' (White, McKay)

Though instrumentals had been a consistent EW&F ingredient, they can be considered as hidden gems in the discography. 'Biyo' (Somali for 'water') could be seen as another reference to the elements that make up the group's name, though water might not quite be what the listener is thinking of when faced with the tracks' hard-edged fusion/funk. The intro sees Dunn making use of sequencer technology, which allows the user to record and playback note patterns at a specific tempo.

A quick drum fill brings in a raucous disco kick and hi-hat pattern, Verdine playing pumping octaves. The horns seem to be building to something, eventually playing a complex line that ends up accented by a drum fill. Verdine and the guitars achieve disco bliss with the next section's four-on-the-floor groove. A strange but funky melody comes in, before the horns start to blast their syncopated notes.

Woolfolk takes an impressive but brief solo over the intro chords. Consecutive players then take solos over the B-section chords, beginning with Graham's slick, bluesy guitar lines. Dunn fires off synth licks before the track verges into an odd sequencer section – programmed notes spitting from the machine in a robotic manner. Eventually, Graham returns, with more Freddie King-style licks.

The kalimba makes an appearance in the B-section's return before a new chord progression appears for Maurice to solo over. Woolfolk takes a lengthy solo that shows incredible emotional and technical dexterity, before the sequencer provides a full stop.

'Burnin' Bush' (Peters)

Written by arranger Jerry Peters – who was brought in towards the end of the album's recording as a replacement for Stepney – 'Burnin' Bush' is another statement of spiritual belief. Peters went on to write for artists like Lee Ritenour and Maxine Nightingale – as well as 'Going in Circles' for The Friends of Distinction featuring former EW&F vocalist Jessica Cleaves – though his main work was in arranging a large amount of the Kalimba Productions output.

Dunn's soothing organ opens with finger cymbals, and Maurice's strong vocal presence suggests a gospel direction. Verdine grooves on a two-note bass riff, while piano and guitar trade licks with the horn section. The string arrangement is magical against this backdrop, and leads into the first verse. With two chords every bar, Maurice sings, 'One glowing look upon a ragged canvas', and how it 'tells the story of our past and present situation'. The group slides into the chorus in a muted rhythm, and Philip responds to Maurice's lines. The dynamics ascend and descend again for verse two. Maurice performs verse three in a preacher-like manner, interspersed with Graham's stinging guitar. This culminates a huge dynamic drop; the track ending with strings – a satisfying ending with huge vision.

All 'N All (1977)

Personnel:
Maurice White: vocals, drums, kalimba
Verdine White: bass, vocals
Ralph Johnson, Fred White: drums
Philip Bailey: vocals, congas, percussion
Al McKay, Johnny Graham: guitar
Larry Dunn: piano, Oberheim and Moog synthesizers
Andrew Woolfolk: tenor saxophone
Louis Satterfield: trombone
Michael Harris, Oscar Brashear: trumpet
Don Myrick: alto, tenor and baritone saxophone
Additional Musicians:
George Bohannon, Garnett Brown: trombone
Roger Bobo: tuba
Chuck Findley, Steve Madaio: trumpet
Alan Robinson, David Duke, Gale Robinson, James McGee, Marilyn Robinson,
Richard Gus Klein: french horn
Eddie del Barrio, Skip Scarborough: piano
Producers: Maurice White, Verdine White, Larry Dunn
Engineers: George Massenburg, Warren Dewey
Studios: Hollywood Sound Recorders, Sunset Sound, Burbank Studios, California
Mastering: Mike Reese at The Mastering Lab
Release date: 21 November 1977
Chart positions: US: 3, US R&B: 1, UK: 13
Running time: 39:04

The success of *Spirit* had solidified EW&F as a *bona fide* pop act, though
bittersweet with the death of friend Charles Stepney. But success wasn't about
to slow down the group's work ethic, and they decided to strike while the
iron was hot.

Maurice was overseeing The Emotions *Rejoice* album for Kalimba
Productions, taking over Stepney's production role, and doing the same
for Deniece Williams' *Song Bird*. Both albums found success, with *Rejoice*
containing the absolute monster hit 'Best Of My Love'. Written by Maurice and
Al McKay, the track hit number 1 on both the Billboard pop and soul charts,
and reached 4 in the UK. Larry Dunn was also stepping out as a producer,
working on jazz/fusion group Caldera's *Sky Islands* album, while Verdine
produced funk act Pocket's minor-hit album *Take it On Up*.

While all this was going on, EW&F were also in the studio, etching out
what would become their next hit album *All 'n All*. With Maurice now firmly
the producer – with assistance from Verdine and Larry – the group moved to
another level of pop production, and an almost impossible level of tightness.
Gone were the days of recording rhythm tracks in the same room at the same

time, as Maurice introduced more stringent overdubbing – though this took a personal toll on the group, as Philip Bailey recalled in *Shining Star*:

> Ironically, the tighter the studio sound got, the more isolated and separate we became as a group. Rather than the band playing together live in the studio like we used to with Charles Stepney, we would often cut our parts separately. As a producer, Maurice was such a taskmaster that guys like Verdine didn't want people watching in the event he made mistakes while laying down his bass parts.

The group was experiencing a culmination effect, snowballing from their years of hard work, turning EW&F into an unstoppable commercial juggernaut. Still, despite the demands of a large mainstream audience, the group continued to push their art forward, and watching *Star Wars* – as well as catching an advance screening of *Close Encounters of the Third Kind* – spurred Maurice to incorporate more Afrofuturism elements into the group's music, artwork and stage presentation. Afrofuturism – with its roots in science fiction and black popular culture – was coming onto its own in the mid-1970s, with pivotal works from authors like Octavia Butler and musicians like Sun Ra.

EW&F turned to Japanese artist Shusei Nagaoka to match the album's artwork to their vision, and he didn't disappoint. The gatefold cover for *All 'N All* was epic to say the least, and grandiose enough to match Maurice' visions of *Close Encounter of the Third Kind*, of which he would recall in *My Life With Earth, Wind & Fire*, 'I was caught up in the symbolism and archetypal meanings. Richard Dreyfuss' character and the mythic elements of communicating with a deity stirred my imagination'. The cover showed a glimmering pyramid shining in the sun atop a monumental structure made from giant pharaoh statues. The back cover and the inner gatefold inspired even more awe. Nagaoka's art set the mood before the album even began, and it's remembered as one of the great album covers of the 1970s.

The group also updated their stage show – fashion designer Bill Whitton giving the group a futuristic new look, and George Faison working on the choreography and special effects. Verdine recalled at soulmusic.com: 'You see, for *us*, *Spirit* represented the end of a particular era for EW&F, and now we're entering a new phase where musical theatre is very much a part of entertainment. That's why we used the services of George Faison in helping put together our new stage show'.

Bailey remembered the gruelling schedule: 'Every morning we would work out with choreographer George Faison, doing callisthenics and rehearsing our dance steps. We would take the afternoon off, then rehearse the music and the show later that night'. The final and maybe most-legendary ingredient of the stage show was magic. They hired magician Doug Henning to work magic tricks into the performance – Verdine famously becoming suspended in mid-air in one of the more notable tricks. Sworn to secrecy, the group never revealed any of Henning's secrets.

When the album came out and the tour rolled around, the hard work all paid off, leading to even greater success. Highly regarded – but often put into contention against *That's the Way of the World* as the group's best album – *All 'n All* is an absolute powerhouse.

'Serpentine Fire' (White, White, Burke)

The half-time feel of 'Serpentine Fire' makes it a force to be reckoned with – a funk behemoth that reached 12 pop and number one in the R&B chart. Written by Maurice and Verdine with keyboardist Sonny Burke, the track is remembered as one of the group's most enduring. The lyric focussed on Maurice's fascination with Kundalini yoga, as he later explained in his autobiography: 'The Kundalini principle has to do with the fluid in the spine. After 29 days, if used properly, it can be converted into a higher consciousness of energy, which means you can step up or step down – it's your choice. It's called a serpent, because, if you tipped the spine out of the body and looked at it, it would look like a serpent, and the fluid is the fire in the spine'.

'Serpentine Fire' has a brief intro featuring Dunn's funky clavinet. Percussion fills out the syncopated kick pattern while the horns accent the end of every bar. A 16th-note buildup leads to the main groove. Maurice and Bailey begin a long note delivery that eventually turns into a descending run. Verdine's bass pops, while the keys and guitar parts play their own rhythmic chord stabs. The horns stand out immediately, playing wildly fast, high bebop lines with extreme precision – looked upon today as some of the finest R&B horn-section playing ever. The sound is clean and precise, with depth. Maurice begins the verse, consisting of a hooky melodic pattern, occasionally joined by Bailey, who highlights certain phrases. His double-tracked chorus vocals are exceptional. Verse two features a great horn countermelody before a stripped-down chorus, slowly building back over the course of the track. It ends with instrumental choruses, with the horns playing the vocal hook into a quick fade.

'Fantasy' (White, White, del Barrio)

'Fantasy' finds the group in science-fiction mode, with some of their most sweeping and cinematic songwriting and arranging to that point. Co-written with Eddie del Barrio (founder of underrated fusion act Caldera, whom Dunn was producing at the time), who also contributes piano to the album, 'Fantasy' was perhaps a bit too adventurous for the time, the single only reached 32, but hitting 12 on the Hot Soul chart. In the UK it was slightly better received, reaching 14.

The multiple stacked vocals became legendary. Bailey recalled in *Shining Star*: "Fantasy' had an airborne feel to it. We became renowned for our soaring group-vocal arrangements, and a song like 'Fantasy' was a terrific vehicle for Maurice and me to multitrack our vocals throughout the verses. Laying them down in the studio was a painstaking process, but well worth it'.

The intro – fit for extraterrestrial royalty – makes way for a fascinating groove. There's no cracking snare, just a rim shot with flourishes of percussion all around. The guitar and bass play the iconic guitar line, and Bailey brings in the science-fiction verse.

Take a ride in the sky
On our ship Fantasi
All your dreams will come true
Right away

The chorus offers a new rising vocal melody, ending in a crescendo with horn lines sailing over a suspended chord. After the second chorus, comes the bridge/refrain, which is so strong it virtually acts as a second unique chorus. The sweeping strings and tight horns blend with the band in an astonishing way. Maurice's low vocal is dominant in the mix, contrasting with Bailey's high work. In a daring arrangement, once the band have reintroduced and replayed the intro section, the track cuts instantly to the last few notes/words of the chorus. Pulled off without a hitch using a tape edit, this type of arrangement would give EW&F the edge over their friendly competition at the time.

The remainder has a slightly different vocal mix and now-legendary Bailey vocal responses. There's an upward key change, and Bailey begins minor licks that perfectly suit the feel. As the lavish arrangement begins to fade, it's clear the listener has heard one of EW&F's finest moments. 'Fantasy' is the aural equivalent of the album artwork – musically cementing the group's concept.

'In The Marketplace (Interlude)' (White)
The kalimba-playing here appropriately evokes a marketplace, with overdubbed, cascading notes and vocals.

'Jupiter' (White, White, Bailey, Dunn)
It's no exaggeration to say 'Jupiter' is one of the hardest-funking tracks of all time, as Larry Dunn would describe to *The Atlantic* 'The rhythm on it made me say, 'who does that?' It had some serious funk on it'. Demonstrating some of the group's tightest work yet; the groove threatening to take off like one of the space shuttles pictured in the artwork. McKay and Verdine lead the way with a stellar riff, soon picked up by the horn section. A slight pause and a blast of horns heralds the arrival of the main sequence. McKay attacks the chords with vigour, Verdine's riveting bass line is slightly reminiscent of Weather Report's fretless-bass player Jaco Pastorious, and the track may be The Phenix Horns' finest moment. Their stuttering back-and-forth notes are impossibly funky and locked in airtight with the hi-hat.

The verse lyric refers to Jupiter as a being – possibly the Roman god of the sky. Innocently looking for the moon, Maurice is met with a sight that would terrify some:

Need was there to tell someone of my discovery
15 seconds later, a light appeared in front of me
To my surprise there stood a man with age and mystery
His name was Jupiter and came to visit me

Bailey sings the chorus melody, sounding as smooth as silk over the harsh backing. Then it switches gear for a series of chord changes. 'We will wait for your return in the by and by', Bailey sings to the protagonist. The band swiftly returns to the opening section, before heading to verse two, as the tale of the extraterrestrial encounter continues. After the second chorus, a series of bebop riffs occur, the key fluctuating as the group deftly navigates complex waters. After the dizzying section, the chorus brings the track back to Earth. The group vamps out on this until the fade-out – the hard funk of 'Jupiter' bulldozing all in its wake.

'Love's Holiday' (White, Scarborough)
This solid soul track provides a reprieve from the funk onslaught. A drum fill and jazz-chord accents introduce the song, Verdine and Maurice in the pocket. Maurice sings in an assured ballad style, drawing the listener in, bringing the verse to a rousing end before crooning through the chorus. The second go-around has Bailey singing more often, complemented by a sly horn arrangement.
    The intro's vocal section is extended and used as a bridge of sorts, before Maurice repeats the chorus, this time with added gusto, his vocals bringing the track to a climax, before a new chord progression takes it out. McKay's guitar playing is another high point here, as are Bailey's panned, rhythmic vocals. Maurice sounds as passionate as ever, trading licks with Graham's hot solo as the track fades.

'Brazilian Rhyme (Interlude)' (White, Nascimento)
Side one's last track races by in just over a minute, but doesn't stop 'Brazilian Rhyme (Interlude)' from being one of their catchiest pieces. Interestingly, future CD releases and streaming platforms would find the track titled 'Beijo (Interlude). Bailey puts on a showcase for vocalists interested in multitracking, all with no lyrics as such, just vocalisations such as the intro 'ba dup's'. Dunn plays smooth Fender Rhodes chords while finger clicks hold down the rhythm. After multiple bars, the rhythm that comes in is irresistible. 'Beijo' has an amazing drum sound, each kick and snare sounding immaculate and daring the listener not to move. The horn section hovers in the background while Verdine pulls out some impressive lines, hitting his signature high vibrato to great effect. A guitar solo begins just as the

track fades out. A highly impressive halfway mark, and possibly the greatest interlude of them all.

'I'll Write A Song For You' (Bailey, McKay, Beckmeier)
Side two opens with softly-picked acoustic guitar. McKay and fellow guitarist Steve Beckmeier wrote the music, and Bailey brought a tender romantic lyric. It's one of his all-time great vocals, and even if the somewhat-saccharine style isn't to everyone's taste, his performance is something to marvel at. Soaring strings add to the sweetness, and verse two sees the arrival of the bass and drums, picking up the dynamic.

The most harmonic section is perhaps the brief bridge at two minutes in. Using more jazz-like chords, the sound is an unexpected delight. It appears again after the third chorus, with a vocal break for Bailey, and a new melody. Here he responds to the upped groove intensity with some incredible improvised licks. His voice has an intense grit as the horns join in, and the track soon fades out. 'I'll Write A Song For You' certainly makes an impression, even if just for Bailey's rousing performance.

'Magic Mind' (White, White, Bailey, Dunn, McKay, White)
'Magic Mind' is a true group collaboration. Larry Dunn later recalled to *The Atlantic*: 'Some of the stuff we wrote together – like the song 'Magic Mind' – we just came up with the groove in a little room'.

McKay's tightly-clipped guitar notes stand out in the intro, and the bass and kick drum bounce around, with the horns providing another burst of staccato notes. In the main intro section, the guitar chords funk as hard as ever, accented with horn stabs. Maurice and Philip's vocals are mixed evenly in verse one:

Hey, we heard the news
That someone's crying the blues
'Cause words still go unsaid
As hungry minds are never fed

The inspirational lyric encourages listeners to pursue their hopes and dreams.

The chorus has a mesmerising vocal pattern as the hypnotic rhythm continues. Joined by swelling horns, verse two has extra guitar and drum frills. Rather than having a second chorus, the group dive into a new section, with a funky horn line leading the way to a ladder-like McKay riff. Following a brief verse, there's a section with hot solo licks from McKay. The group finally settles back into the chorus – the lyric apt as they induce a trance-like state.

Take a chance, as you dance in romance
In a trance, to advance and expand

The group is soon dropped out of the mix, leaving only the layered horn arrangement, before the group returns to fade out on the groove.

'Runnin'' (White, Dunn, del Barrio)

The album's second co-write to feature Argentinian pianist Eddie del Barrio, is a high-tech funk/fusion masterpiece. The stellar vocals set it apart from other fusion groups of the time, like Weather Report and Return to Forever, who used fewer vocals and it would quickly become a fan favourite. It took some time to capture in the studio. Philip Bailey recalled in *Shining Star*: 'When we were cutting *All 'N All*'s instrumental jam – a track called 'Runnin'' – we were originally going to perform it with Freddie and Ralph on drums. Somehow though, we couldn't get the rhythm right, so Verdine, Larry, Maurice and I worked on it, and we were cooking on that song! It sounded like something off a CTI record'. (CTI was a jazz label famous for its funky take on the genre.)

Opening with a twisting bebop line, the track moves into one of the group's greatest grooves of all, Maurice's snare work keeping them in check. McKay again plays clipped lines, while Verdine stays relatively relaxed and lets the track breathe. A muted horn line lends a slightly mythical vibe, opening the door for the vocals, with Bailey and White singing in a scat style. The B section features surreal chord changes and more vocal hooks, eventually peaking in an explosion of notes from the drums and keys. Another new section appears, sounding particularly grand, Bailey's vocal melody bringing to mind the dunes of an endless desert.

After repeating, the group breaks into an up-tempo jazz feel, Maurice again demonstrating his drumming expertise. Harris and Myrick trade solos, before the group break down into near-free-jazz territory, Maurice's snare throwing out rolls. The track comes to an end, and we hear voices talking as 'Serpentine Fire' is heard playing on what sounds like a transistor radio in the background.

'Runnin'' is a 1970s fusion essential, from a group that was scaling the top of the pop charts!

'Brazilian Rhyme (Interlude)'(Brant, Nascimento)

A brief and reflective piece and another interlude providing respite from the funk. It sounds something like incidental Disney movie music. Like the earlier track it shares its name with, subsequent CD releases, and streaming platforms, find this track with a different title, in this case 'Brazilian Rhyme (aka Ponta de Areia)'.

'Be Ever Wonderful' (White, Dunn)

'Be Ever Wonderful' begins with the kind of complex brass parts The Phenix horns were now known for. The track is soon shown to be a slow, swung soul number with some jazz changes. The track shows off Dunn's blossoming writing skills, and parts feel like a nod to the group's fallen mentor Charles

Stepney. Larry recalled to *The Atlantic*: 'I came home one night from hanging out at some clubs, and I wasn't really sleepy. It got later and later, and something was coming up. It was raining outside, and I stayed up all night and went into the studio. By noon, I called Maurice and told him I had finished all the music for the song. I played it over the phone and he was like, 'Yeah!''.

Maurice turned in a memorable vocal – a highlight in a career filled with highlights. The chords are melancholy but uplifting, coming across like a big band version of gospel, while the bridge vocal arrangement is stunning in its scope. 'As you live today, what I wanna say/Be ever wonderful in your own sweet way', Maurice intones in the closing lines before an extended B section shows the band pulling out all the stops.

The Best of Earth, Wind & Fire, Vol. 1 (1978)

Personnel:
Maurice White: vocals, drums, kalimba
Verdine White: bass, vocals
Ralph Johnson, Fred White: drums
Philip Bailey: vocals, congas, percussion
Al McKay, Johnny Graham: guitar
Larry Dunn: piano, Oberheim and Moog synthesizers
Andrew Woolfolk: tenor saxophone
Louis Satterfield: trombone
Michael Harris: trumpet
Don Myrick: alto, tenor and baritone saxophone
Rhamlee Michael Davis: trumpet, flugelhorn
Oscar Brashear: trumpet
Producers: Maurice White, Verdine White, Larry Dunn
Engineer: George Massenburg
Mastered by Mark Wilder
Studios: Northstar, Boulder, Colorado ('Got To Get You Into My Life'), The
Complex, Los Angeles, California ('September')
Release date: 23 November 1978
Chart positions: US: 6, R&B: 13, UK: 6
Running time: 40:07
Track Listing:
A1 – Got To Get You Into My Life
A2 – Fantasy
A3 – Can't Hide Love
A4 – Love Music
A5 – Getaway
B1 – That's The Way of The World
B2 – September
B3 – Shining Star
B4 – Reasons
B5 – Sing a Song

There are two reasons for including EW&F's first greatest hits album here.
One reason is their take on The Beatles' 'Got To Get You Into My Life' –
originally released a few months prior on the soundtrack to the infamous
Sgt. Pepper's Lonely Hearts Club Band movie. Reason two is EW&F's all-
conquering and indomitable hit 'September', which further implanted the
group into popular culture, becoming one of the most popular tracks of all
time, coming in at number 63 on *Rolling Stone*'s 2021 list of the greatest ever.
  Maurice had been negotiating further business for Kalimba Productions
when he struck a golden business opportunity. CBS officially offered for him
to operate an imprint label under their umbrella, using the name of one of

America's oldest labels: American Recording Company (ARC). The Kalimba Productions artists would all be on the roster, alongside popular acts like Weather Report and Valerie Carter. Maurice was given an all-in-one office space in Los Angeles, which he named The Complex. The building contained office space, rehearsal rooms, a recording studio and a soundstage.

By the end of 1978, head of Columbia Records Bruce Lundvall informed the group that they were officially on record as the biggest group in the world at the time (taking into account sales, worldwide acceptance, awards and touring statistics.) However, staying on top would be a different story.

'Got To Get You Into My Life' (Lennon, McCartney)

The compilation begins with the classic Beatles song from their album *Revolver*. Recorded on tour while in Boulder, Colorado, EW&F only had 48 hours to record and mix it in order to submit it for the *Sgt. Pepper's Lonely Hearts Club Band* soundtrack. Featuring other acts such as Peter Frampton, The Bee Gees and Aerosmith, the fantastical storyline involving Peter Frampton battling evil members of the music industry, the film bombed upon release, but is looked upon as something of a cult favourite.

EW&F's take makes no rush to get through the arrangement, opening with quarter-notes clusters that set the tone before dropping back to finger clicks, Fender Rhodes, Graham and McKay's guitar licks and some squealing horn accents. In the opening chorus, Maurice takes his voice from a near-whisper to a soul-powered belt, before the group replays the intro. The groove is instantly danceable, Johnson's drums swinging as Bailey and Maurice scat with the horn section. Maurice takes the verses, ending each phrase with a show of power, while Bailey's unmistakable falsetto joins for the pre-chorus, but is just a tease, as the verse reappears. A full-band chorus is next, Verdine really laying it down. Graham's rock solos fit the track to a tee before multiple choruses lead to the fade-out.

It's a joyous take on what was an already-classic song, and this version was heaped with accolades. George Martin himself informed Maurice that he wished the group had recorded the entire *Sgt. Pepper's Lonely Hearts Club Band* soundtrack. Maurice would later recall the track fondly in *My Life With Earth, Wind & Fire*:

We cooked a jazzy, greasy Memphis groove with a touch of big-band swing. Verdine could've walked the bass line like he was playing upright bass with Count Basie, it was swinging that hard. I think it's one of Verdine's best bass performances on record, and according to Paul McCartney, it's his favourite Beatles cover.

'September' (White, McKay, Willis)

'September' is a pure musical distillation of the EW&F philosophy. Radiating the joy and positivity the band fostered in every facet of their lifestyles, it became a blockbuster. Al McKay formulated the demo at his home studio, two distinct chord progressions that would be discussed by musicians for decades to come. He later recalled to *Classic Pop* magazine: 'I did an 8-track and brought it for Maurice, and he loved it. That was the only time I got close to recording some music. What you hear on 'September' today, the opening, that's all guitars mostly – I did all of those. Maurice loved it'.

Verdine introduced Maurice to young songwriter Allee Willis (who later worked with artists such as Sister Sledge, Cyndi Lauper and Pet Shop Boys. One of her biggest claims to fame is the Emmy-nominated theme song to sitcom *Friends*). Willis remembered in an interview with *americansongwriter. com*: 'When I walked in, the band was working on the intro, and I thought, 'Please let this be the one they want me to work on'. It was the happiest-sounding thing I had ever heard!'. Maurice explained to Willis that the song would be the last piece in a trilogy written by him and McKay (the others being 'Best Of My Love' and 'Sing A Song'), loosely based on the same rhythmic feel. White and Willis spent about a month working on the lyric, with Willis not too sure about the chorus 'ba de ya' vocals, but Maurice stood firm on the line. Beginning with McKay's hooky, multi-layered guitars backed with a pumping cowbell, the track soon kicks in with a catchy horn line. Tom Washington – who frequently worked with Maurice on Kalimba sessions – came up with a horn arrangement that suited the track perfectly.

The vocal begins with the iconic lines:

Do you remember the 21st night of September?
Love was changing the minds
Pretenders while chasing the clouds away

Fans the world over came to recognise September 21st as Earth, Wind & Fire day, and the group have sometimes augmented the date with the release of a new film clip or remix of the track.

Once the chorus comes, there's no way the listener can escape the hook. The 'ba de ya' line would be sung by people around the world at concerts, sporting events, rallies, weddings, parties and just about any event that could be held, becoming a rallying cry for happiness. White and Bailey sing a different hook after the chorus, before the horns play a series of notes like fireworks. Verse two keeps the mood up, the horns repeating their post-chorus line, and Maurice keeping the vocals as upbeat as possible. In chorus two, Bailey provides a marvellous countermelody to the main line, which is picked up for every following chorus. Maurice keeps the third verse brief, and the chorus repeats until the fade-out, the Phenix Horns eventually kicking things up a notch for added excitement.

The single reached eight on the pop chart – having a lengthy stay – and reached three in the UK. With the release of 'September', Earth, Wind & Fire cemented their reputation as one of the seventies' premier funk acts.

I Am (1979)

Personnel:
Maurice White: vocals, drums, kalimba
Verdine White: bass, vocals
Ralph Johnson, Fred White: drums
Philip Bailey: vocals, congas, percussion
Al McKay, Johnny Graham: guitar
Larry Dunn: piano, Oberheim and Moog synthesizers
Andrew Woolfolk: tenor saxophone
Louis Satterfield: trombone
Michael Harris: trumpet
Don Myrick: alto, tenor and baritone saxophone
Rhamlee Michael Davis: trumpet, flugelhorn
Additional Musicians:
Fred Jackson Jr., Herman Riley, Jerome Richardson: saxophone
Benjamin Powell, William Reichenbach, Garnett Brown, George Bohanon,
Maurice Spears: trombone
Bobby Bryant, Jerry Hey, Steve Madaio: trumpet
Barbara Korn, Marilyn Richardson, Richard Perissi, Sidney Muldrow: french horn
Janice Gower: concertmaster
Steve Lukather, Marlo Henderson: guitar
Billy Meyers, David Foster, Eddie del Barrio: keyboards
Producers: Maurice White, Al McKay ('Boogie Wonderland')
Engineers: George Massenburg, Tom Perry, Craig Widby, Ross Pallone
Studios: Hollywood Sound Recorders, Sunset Sound, Davlen Sound, Los Angeles,
California
Mastering: Mike Reese
Release date: 9 June 1979
Chart positions: US: 3, R&B: 1, UK: 5
Running time: 37:40

Maurice now turned his attention to maintaining the group's hard-won spot.
In his view, this meant changing things – the biggest shift being excluding the
other members (particularly McKay and Dunn) from the songwriting. Maurice
had a fully-realised vision for the new album, and it was to come at the
expense of certain EW&F members, driving a wedge between them. Maurice
later recalled in *My Life With Earth, Wind & Fire*: 'I, David Foster and Allee
Willis wrote the majority of the *I Am* album. The other writers were Eddie Del
Barrio, Jon Lind (who co-wrote 'Boogie Wonderland' with Allee) and a young
kid by the name of Bill Meyers. The limited number of writers is one of the
components that made *I Am* a focused record. But that focus came with a
serious price'.
    Maurice's eye for talent cannot be argued. David Foster was a young
Canadian pianist and songwriter who found a career in Los Angeles, picking

59

up session work with George Harrison and Guthrie Thomas. Foster had scored big in 1978 with Cheryl Lynn's 'Got To Be Real', which he wrote with Lynn and Toto's David Paich. Foster also happened to be a big EW&F fan. A mutual friend passed Foster's contact details to Maurice, informing him that Foster had a song for the group. That song turned out to be the now-classic 'After The Love Has Gone' – a co-write with session guitarist Jay Graydon and future Chicago member Bill Champlin.

More session musicians were brought in, as Maurice seeked to keep the group sounding fresh. Notable additional names on the album included guitarists Steve Lukather (Toto) and Marlo Henderson, Bill Meyers and Foster on keys, and Paulinho Da Costa and Richard Lepore on percussion. Maurice also brought in The Emotions for backing vocals on 'Boogie Wonderland'.

'In The Stone' (White, Willis, Foster)

'In The Stone' is a remarkable statement, setting the tone for the rest of the album. Production-wise, *I Am* might be the culmination of Maurice's vision. Every instrument shines. The introduction sounds regal, the drums are tight and punchy, and every instrument has its own area in the mix. The track still sounds fresh today – a testament to the knowledge and work of Maurice White and George Massenburg. The lengthy intro has horn parts to die for, and great drum fills. The stakes are even higher, with the entry of skanking guitar chords, and strings heightening the tension. The groove that comes in is phenomenal – Verdine locked-in airtight, with possibly his best bass tone yet. Intricate piano and guitar lines dance around, and the percussion sounds in the left channel are the opening argument in why this track – and the entire album – may be best heard through high-quality headphones.

Maurice's double-tracked verse vocal is restrained and soulful.

> I found that love provides the key
> Unlocks the heart and souls of you and me
> Love will learn to sing your song
> Oh yeah, love is written in the stone

Bailey's falsetto enters in the chorus, which has a new set of chords and a slightly altered rhythm. McKay pedals funky octaves in the right channel, the string section adding a rising and falling line that allows the track to breathe. In the second chorus, a marvellous New Orleans-style descending horn line is added. The band drops out briefly for the refrain, the first chord cycle consisting of only Foster's piano, Dunn's synth and Maurice's vocals. Unbelievable horn lines swirl around the lines 'Never my darling, never you'll be alone', creating a mountain of undisputed R&B power. It ends with a tight group accent before a short uncredited musical passage with a solid four-on-the-floor groove and calming kalimba playing.

'Can't Let Go' (White, Willis, Meyers)
'Can't Let Go' begins with another of The Phenix Horns' intricate lines, trumpets sitting atop like a crown jewel. The up-tempo rhythm has a swagger that matches Maurice's vocal. Funky guitar parts help propel it all. The first chorus rolls in at around 23 seconds, and what a chorus it is – shining quick and bright, spanning Maurice's vocal range, ending on a breathy low note.

Bailey is brought in for the second verse, his entrancing vocals strategically placed. Following the second chorus, a short bridge disappears quickly as another chorus flies by. After a brief return to the intro, Dunn plays a synth melody, and the horns and vocals eventually enter, continuing to the fade-out.

'After The Love Has Gone' (Foster, Champlin, Graydon)
Guitarist Jay Graydon and Foster wrote the music, and Bill Champlin the lyric for this ballad which was as strong as anything the group had written. It begins with Foster's inspirational chords, soon joined by strings and synth. The verse has jazz-informed chords over which Maurice sings his tale of love gone sour, and he really nails his part. The pre-chorus begins innocently enough, bringing in bass, drums and guitar quietly, until a sudden key change sees the melody swerve off track, and Bailey steps in to handle the part. The drums groove in the chorus, smooth horns surrounding the soaring vocal melody.

The second chorus eventually sweeps through six-chord accents, until settling on one for an immense key change. Bailey rises to the occasion with a classic vocal, before Woolfolk plays a sweet sax solo. In *Shining Star*, Bailey recalled the difficulties surrounding the track:

'After The Love' was not an easy piece to sing, and from a strictly technical standpoint, you could make the argument that it is flawed. Its overambitious architecture demands a multi-octave range, and, theoretically, to do it justice, one person can't perform the entire song alone. Maybe it should've been sung by a female vocalist with a higher and wider gospel range. Luckily, EWF had the necessary combined range and vocal firepower to handle it. We solved the inherent problems in the song's structure, by having Maurice do the verses, with me singing the chorus, enabling us to capture the breadth of its notes and emotions.

Andrew Woolfolk performs a stunning solo over the outro, breezing through smooth lines in his be-bop-inspired style, and occasionally spitting out fiery, stuttering runs. Woolfolk continues playing as the group eventually fades out – indicating that the solo was tracked once both songs were edited together- revealing the strings' stirring arrangement on its own. This quickly makes way for the groove of 'Let Your Feelings Show', the track bleeding into each other in a well-thought-out way.

The song won the 1980 Grammy for Best R&B Song, and is one of the biggest hits in the EW&F catalogue. Champlin recalled writing the song, in conversation with *songwriteruniverse.com*:

'After The Love Has Gone' turned out to be a great thing. At the time, David was working as a session guy for Maurice White and Earth, Wind & Fire. And while they were rolling the tape back, Maurice went, 'Whoa, what's that? I gotta hear it'. So I think he had a cassette of my version, and he said, 'If Bill will agree to not release it on his record, we'll cut it and release it', and I went, 'Okay, let's do that. Let's make that happen'.

'Let Your Feelings Show' (White, Willis, Foster)
The rhythm guitar and bass here merge with the percussion to create a rhythmic monster before the horns bring everything to a screeching halt with only kick underneath. The lyric finds Maurice seemingly lost in love:

Laughing into midnight, love will be my guide
We approach the morning, feeling good inside
Baby, gonna let my feelings show
Every day, gonna learn to love you more

Toto guitarist Steve Lukather is heard in the chorus playing line to counter Bailey's chorus part. Stacked horn lines offer a listening alternative to the vocals, while not detracting. After repeating the verse and chorus, it drops down to a skanking rhythmic guitar pattern, drums and percussion. The group jam out into the fade, ending side one.

'Boogie Wonderland' (Willis, Lind)
The side-two opener was an out-and-out disco track. Originally 'Boogie Wonderland' began life as an ARC Records track McKay was producing for The Curtis Brothers. However, Maurice felt that the group wasn't quite getting the feel down, and soon came to the realisation that he could do the track justice. EW&F soon began their arrangement, The Emotions brought in to supply their exceptional vocal harmonies. Bailey recalled the process in *Shining Star*:

When we agreed to cut 'Boogie Wonderland', Maurice and I decided that if we were actually going to record a disco number, we would pull out all the stops and do it our way. The arrangements and orchestrations were punchy – our response to the dreaded disco era. It was Al and Maurice' idea to use a slamming female trio – The Emotions, that had just joined Reese' new ARC label – to augment the groove. Influenced by German producer Giorgio Moroder's immaculate beat-driven hits with Donna Summer, we took it a step further and featured three layers of vocals – with Maurice singing lead, plus The Emotions, and my voice added to the top of the heap.

A surprisingly complicated arrangement engages the listener over a thumping disco feel, and The Emotions arrive quickly, harmonising on 'Dance, boogie wonderland'. Maurice's slick verse vocal masks the darkness of Allee Willis' lyric, which counteracted the happy-go-lucky vibe of disco.

Midnight creeps so slowly
Into hearts of men who need more than they get
Daylight deals a bad hand
To a woman who has laid too many bets

A magical-sounding bridge arrives out of nowhere, Dunn's synth bass thumping underneath The Emotions' vocals. Bailey emits a powerhouse run, nailing a high note before returning the song back to the chorus. Sweet strings and frantic horn lines foreshadow the next vocal hook. The percussion and horns increase the intensity, before string lines unfold. The bridge returns, and Bailey manages to impress even more than the last time, before the choruses close the track.

'Boogie Wonderland' was a worldwide hit, climbing to six in the US, four in the UK, and reaching the top ten in Europe, Australia and New Zealand.

'Star' (White, del Barrio, Willis)

Beginning with smooth sounding synth, the group's sci-fi influences are on full display. Strings softly enhance the atmosphere, until horns and a kick drum announce the groove's arrival. The incredibly joyous 'Star' leans heavily on its stomping rhythm. Philip Bailey begins the verse at the one-minute mark, the descending melody demonstrating jazz-like intervals. Bailey and Maurice sound relaxed throughout as they sing 'Star bright, star light' – a play on the old nursery rhyme. Bailey stamps his personality on the track, and his vocal tone is top-notch. Another verse and chorus set up the outro – a long solo section for Louis Satterfield, with the Phenix Horns in trad-jazz style.

'Star' was a minor hit in the US, and beloved by the group's fans. It reached 64 in the US but fared better in the UK, hitting 16 there.

'Wait' (White, Foster, Willis)

The album's second ballad features all the hallmarks of what would become David Foster's familiar writing style. Striding piano sits atop the 12/8 rhythm, a thick overdriven guitar supplying a melody the horns soon have an answer for. Maurice handles the verse vocal, Bailey entering with tight, syncopated harmonies, horns later joining for extra emphasis.

Though not essential, 'Wait' is still a great example of EW&F musicianship, and helps to break up the album's pacing.

'Rock That!' (White, Foster)

This more-rock instrumental featured distorted guitar sounding more like the group's early days, though with less Hendrix fuzz. A great string arrangement bridges the intro to the next section, Dunn pounding out the piano rhythm. Johnny Graham takes a bluesy solo, weaving around the string lines underneath. Steve Lukather brings in some hard-rock riffing, and the Phenix Horns follow him through several key changes before settling back into the groove. A new section and new riff arrive, with a complex horn arrangement leading to the fade-out.

'Rock That!' sits well on the album, and its rock elements were to creep into the group's future work.

'You And I' (White, Willis, Foster)

Climbing and then rapidly falling, this intro is a testament to the group's sheer power at this stage. The verse feels almost unexpected after the intro, and the serene funk makes a great bed for the vocal. Jazz guitar pulses lie underneath the horns, Verdine grabs a high vibrato note, while the drums and horns are perfectly in sync to usher in the pre-chorus. The chorus rhythm switches from the straight 16ths to a swung groove, the chords sounding uplifting compared to the mysterious verse progression. Horns lead to a brief bridge section. 'We must trust the dark/Showing us the stars/We must trust the rain and open up our hearts' Maurice intones before the chorus returns as the album finale. From the 1986 European CD reissue onwards, the track also features an extra 30 seconds of music for completionists.

Right: The original EW&F lineup, with vocalist Sherry Scott (1972). (*mauricewhite.com*)

Left: This press shot shows the group at the top of their game, and in memorable stage wear. (*mauricewhite.com*)

Right: The group's most beloved lineup is back for one last performance at their induction into the Rock and Roll Hall of Fame in 2000. (*Kevin Mazur, mauricewhite.com*)

Left: Earth, Wind & Fire's self-titled debut (1971). (*Warner Bros.*)

Right: The group's second and final album for Warner Bros. *The Need of Love* (1971) saw them take a step forward from their debut. (*Warner Bros.*)

Left: *Last Days and Time* (1972) saw the group begin a long and fruitful relationship with Columbia Records. (*Columbia Records*)

Right: Album art for *Head To The Sky* (1973), with Jessica Cleaves prominently featured. (*Columbia Records*)

Left: Album art for *Open Our Eyes* (1974). (*Columbia Records*)

Right: Album art for the group's breakthrough album, *That's The Way of The World* (1975). (*Columbia Records*)

Left: *Gratitude* showcases the group both in performance and in the studio. (*Columbia Records*)

Right: The album *Spirit* (1976) was intended as a tribute to a fallen friend, songwriter, arranger and producer Charles Stepney. (*Columbia Records*)

Left: The iconic album art for *All 'N All* (1977), was created by Japanese artist Shusei Nagaoka. (*Columbia Records*)

Right: The group's first compilation, *The Best of Earth, Wind & Fire Volume 1* (1978) contained brand new hit 'September', which would go on to become one of their most beloved songs. (*Columbia Records*)

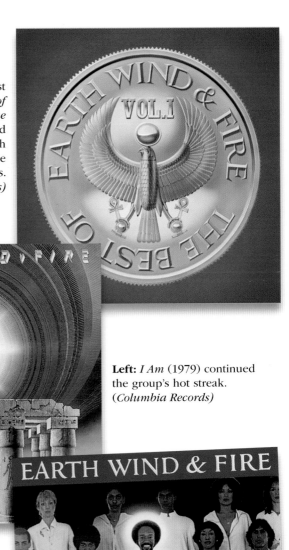

Left: *I Am* (1979) continued the group's hot streak. (*Columbia Records*)

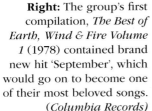

Right: Double album *Faces* (1980) would see a dip in popularity for the group. (*Columbia Records*)

Left: *Open Our Eyes* (1974) promo shot. By this stage, the group's classic, core lineup was fully formed. (*mauricewhite.com*)

Right: A press shot of the group taken for *All 'N All*, considered by some to be the group's greatest work. (*mauricewhite.com*)

Left: The classic lineup of Earth, Wind & Fire, the group Philip Bailey would describe as 'commercial fusion'. (*mauricewhite.com*)

Right: Maurice White in the 'Boogie Wonderland' clip. Promotional videos would become more and more important to the group as the 1980s approached. (*Columbia Records*)

Left: Phillip sings 'Fantasy' live at the height of the group's powers.

Right: Phillip and Phenix Horns member Don Myrick, who, tragically, was shot dead in 1993.

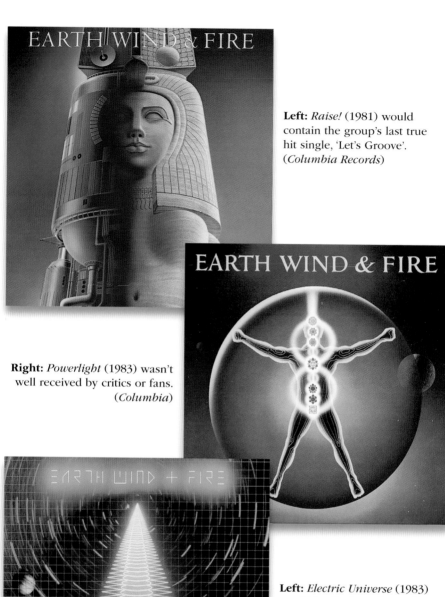

Left: *Raise!* (1981) would contain the group's last true hit single, 'Let's Groove'. (*Columbia Records*)

Right: *Powerlight* (1983) wasn't well received by critics or fans. (*Columbia*)

Left: *Electric Universe* (1983) would be the last album of the group's first run, before a five-year hiatus, during which time Bailey would begin a successful run as a solo artist. (*Columbia Records*)

Right: Reunion album *Touch The World* (1987) would find the band updating its sound for the late 1980s market. (*Columbia Records*)

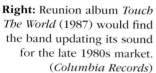

Left: *Heritage* (1990) would perform so poorly that it saw Columbia drop the group after a long relationship. (*Columbia*)

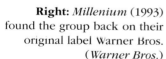

Right: *Millenium* (1993) found the group back on their original label Warner Bros. (*Warner Bros.*)

Left: *In The Name of Love* (1997) was originally released in Japan the year before as *Avatar*. (*Rhino Records*)

Right: The original artwork for *The Promise* (2003), which reached number 19 on the *Billboard* R&B Charts. (*Kalimba Productions*)

Left: *Illumination* (2005) was something of a comeback for the group, featuring guest appearances by acts such as Floetry, will.i.am and Kenny G. It reached 32 on the *Billboard* Hot 200 chart. (*Sanctuary Records*)

Right: The cover of acclaimed album *Now, Then & Forever* (2013), a return to form for the Philip Bailey-led incarnation of the group. It is also their last album of original music to date. (*Legacy Recordings/Sony Music*)

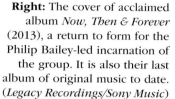

Left: EW&F helped spread some festive cheer with the Christmas-themed album *Holiday.* (2014) (*Legacy Recordings/Sony Music*)

Right: The group's last compilation release with Columbia Records was the three-disc career overview *The Eternal Dance.* (*Columbia Records*)

Above: The Whites warming up with members of the Phenix Horns. (*mauricewhite.com*)

Below: Maurice White performing live. (*mauricewhite.com*)

Above: The group would return in 1987, although several notable members would sit out on the reunion. (*mauricewhite.com*)

Below: The group pictured in performance from their *Live in Japan* (1990) home video release. (*Eagle Rock Records*)

Above: The Phillip Bailey-led incarnation of the group live in 2002. (*Getty*)

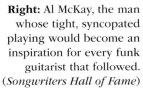

Right: Al McKay, the man whose tight, syncopated playing would become an inspiration for every funk guitarist that followed. (*Songwriters Hall of Fame*)

Right: Verdine White in action, renowned as one of the greatest bassists to ever get funky. (*Tom Beetz*)

Above: Known as a gifted vocalist, Philip Bailey's solo work is also world-renowned. (*Jabari Jacobs/Universal Music Group*)

Left: The movie poster for Sig Shore's *That's The Way of The World* (1975). The movie would bomb, but the soundtrack would go on to be considered an all-time classic. (*Sig Shore Productions*)

Right: Shusei Nagaoka's striking gatefold artwork for *I Am* (1979). (*Columbia Records*)

Faces (1980)

Personnel:
Maurice White: vocals, drums, kalimba
Verdine White: bass, vocals
Ralph Johnson, Fred White: percussion
Philip Bailey: vocals, congas, percussion
Al McKay, Johnny Graham: guitar
Larry Dunn: piano, synthesizer, programming
Andrew Woolfolk: tenor saxophone
Louis Satterfield: trombone
Michael Harris: trumpet
Don Myrick: alto, tenor and baritone saxophone
Rhamlee Michael Davis: trumpet, flugelhorn
Additional Musicians:
William Reichenbach, Fred Wesley, George Bohanon, Jeff Clayton: trombone
Fred Jackson Jr, Lawrence Williams: saxophone, flute
Alan Robinson, Arthur Maebe, George Price, Marilyn Robinson, Vincent de Rosa: french horn
Bobby Bryant, Chuck Findley, Gary E. Grant, Jerry Hey, Nolan Smith Jr., Steve Madaio: trumpet
John Johnson: tuba
Paulinho da Costa: percussion
Assa Drori, Harris Goldman, Janice Gower: concertmasters
Steve Lukather, Marlo Henderson: guitar
David Foster, Garry Glenn, Jerry Peters: keyboards
Producer: Maurice White
Engineers: George Massenburg, Ken Fowler, Ray Gonzalez, Wally Heider, Geoff Ions, Steve Jackson, Jeff Borgeson, Bob Wolstein
Studios: ARC, Royce Hall UCLA, Davlen Sound, Filmways, Hollywood, CA; Air Studios, Montserrat, West Indies
Mastering: Wayne A. Dickson
Released date: 14 October 1980
Chart positions: US: 10, US soul: 2, UK: 10
Running time: 1:06:10

The mammoth *I Am* tour showed off the group's pop-star status, and a young David Copperfield was hired to work on the magic tricks and disappearing acts which left audiences with their mouths open. But Maurice found himself under immense pressure from the success and all it entailed. His record label ARC was going through a rough patch, and he wasted no time in returning to the studio looking for a hit.

The songwriting process was opened up to outside writers even more, and numerous studio musicians (including nearly every Toto member) were brought in. Dunn and McKay, in particular, were upset with the situation and

65

began to speak out against Maurice in recording sessions, as Bailey recalled in *Shining Star*:

> McKay's presence was felt less and less, and through his discontent, I could see cracks in the band's infrastructure. Al was unhappy that there was now a very evident, large financial abyss between Maurice and the other band members, and he felt that the rest of us weren't getting paid enough. He would often try to gauge the other guys' reaction over the matter, and once pulled Larry Dunn aside and said, 'You know, if we all pull together, we can get on Maurice and nip this whole inequality thing in the bud!'.

McKay's tension soon came to a head, though Maurice later admitted, 'As much as I didn't like the conflict between Al and me, I couldn't help but believe that it contributed to the heat of the recordings. Our fiery rhythm section still prevailed'. Bailey was also a witness to the impact of the new decade's incoming technology, and describes David Foster introducing the brand new LinnDrum to Maurice:

> ''This is the future of recording', David told Reese, and with one press of a button, they marvelled as a clear, piercing and snappy synthesized snare-drum hit emanated from the digital machine. Maurice and Foster were fascinated with the device, and Maurice would use it for our next album *Faces*. From that point on, technology would profoundly influence Maurice's methods of production, and the new era of drum machines and polyphonic synthesizers would greatly affect our communal vibe as a studio band'.

The group had accrued enough material for the upcoming album *Faces* to be a double LP. Maurice sought to replicate the soothing environment of Caribou Ranch – the ghost town where they'd recorded earlier albums – flying the core members to Sir George Martin's AIR Studios at Montserrat, where they recorded with their usual engineer George Massenburg. However, to Maurice's dismay, the close quarters just inflamed the situation with McKay. After recording the basic rhythm tracks, they flew back to California, finishing the album in four studios (including The Complex), using numerous engineers. After impressing on *I Am*, trumpet player Jerry Hey wrote the group horn arrangements from here on.

Maurice also sought further funding by establishing corporate partnerships. EW&F signed a $500,000 contract with Panasonic to promote their new boombox cassette players, and appear in the advertisements to help promote album sales. The album's lead single 'Let Me Talk' only reached 44 in the US and 29 in the UK. The next two singles fared no better – 'You' reaching 48 in the US, and 'And Love Goes On' stumbling to 59 – however, like the album itself, they fared better on the Hot R&B and Hot Soul charts, 'You' hitting number 10 and 'And Love Goes On' reaching 15.

Nonetheless, the album received a mostly positive critical reaction, and most fans regard it as one of the group's finest albums. The recording techniques begun in earnest with *Spirit* might've reached their zenith with *I Am*, but *Faces* certainly saw the band holding steady, even if its length discouraged some casual listeners. Something of an underrated gem, the album has plenty of dance-floor fillers, and some surprises.

The situation with McKay reached boiling point on the subsequent tour, the guitarist quitting halfway through, though Maurice claimed McKay was fired for failing to turn up to a show. In a bizarre turn of events, McKay was replaced by the man he'd originally replaced: Roland Bautista. McKay's presence was missed; however, Maurice later recalled, 'Roland was good, but he wasn't Al. Al's departure from the band was a big loss, and the end of an era'.

'Let Me Talk' (White, White, Dunn, McKay, Johnson)

The lead single and opening track is a slightly odd, percussion-filled slice of funky bliss. Larry Dunn's synth programming is taken to new heights in the intro, spitting out notes like welding sparks. McKay's layered guitars keep the track moving, the horns laying down some excellent lines, while a squeaky synth patch pops its head out every now and then. Maurice's vocals are snappy, him giving responses to his 'I stand tall, let me talk' hook. The lyric is a criticism of capitalism, and extols the virtues of staying true to oneself.

The bridge sees the arrival of revolving chords and a heavy synth bass to thicken up the bottom end while Bailey's lead vocal flies above on the opposite end of the sonic spectrum. The chorus returns, the drum rhythm stays and McKay plays a riff like only he can, combining with the synth bass in a tangled web of harmony. The Phenix Horns shine, as usual, their tight compressed trumpet sound the cherry on the cake. The verse three lyric asks a question of the listener:

Now where does it all lead to?
I'm sure the question flows
Through many minds around the world
I'm sure nobody knows

'Let Me Talk' is an interesting choice for a lead single, and is great evidence of the group's artistry, even in the face of growing division from within.

'Turn It Into Something Good' (White, Howard, Carter)

Co-written with singer Valerie Carter, 'Turn it Into Something Good' brings the tempo down, but the groove *up*. Carter had been mentored by Little Feat's Lowell George, leading to a string of successful solo albums. Her first album, *Just a Stone's Throw Away* included the song 'City Lights' written by Maurice, Verdine, Fred, Al and Larry.

The smooth chord progression and steady rhythm are augmented by a shaker. Soaring strings and horns lead to Maurice's verse, where he sings with power and passion. Bailey joins for the pre-chorus, before an ascending chord progression leads to both singing in the chorus. The chorus sees the track out, bringing to close a great exercise in smooth funk, leaning towards Carter's West Coast AOR style.

'Pride' (White, White, White, Dunn, McKay, Bailey)

'Pride' begins with McKay's strangely-effected guitar (a combination of compression and wah) surrounded by The Phenix Horns, and synthesizer fills the low end, doubling the bass in places. While the band pauses, the horn line descends into the next groove, the heavy synth announcing that the 1980s have arrived.

The track finds the group experimenting with studio techniques more than ever – such as the reversed guitar and horns. A forward-rolling horn line, stabs with the drums over the vocals, the lyric telling of the positive factors that pride can help reinforce. Verse two introduces a vocal countermelody before the instrumental section blasts off. Complex bebop lines call back and forth, extra percussion driving the groove even harder, until all instruments involved play an airtight riff that crashes into the next verse. Kalimba soon joins the mix – a nice, earthy surprise over the modern production. Maurice takes a solo, before the accents appear and the band play a final riff to end, a spacey synth pad with slow delay, leading to the next song.

'You' (White, Foster, Russell)

Brenda Russell was just beginning her solo career after time mostly spent working with her former husband, Brian Russell. The pair sang backing vocals for artists like Elton John, Neil Sedaka and Robert Palmer.

This opens with Foster's acoustic piano and Dunn's Fender Rhodes together, with horns, strings and rhythm section slowly washing in like an ocean wave. The lyric is reasonably typical fare for such songs at the time.

She was naive, and never knew
Back against the world, her dreams came true
There is a mirror in her eyes
All the world with cherry-painted skies

Foster pumps out 8th notes on the piano, as Maurice and Philip sail high above with breathy vocals, an out-of-the-blue key change followed with expert skill. A jazz-like transition brings the verse back. An extra horn riff is brought in over the next chorus, increasing the interest level. A Woolfolk sax solo brings the track to its peak, the chorus repeating to the fade.

While certainly qualifying for the Adult Contemporary tag, the track rises above the cliches of the genre, delivering something genuinely stirring.

'Sparkle' (White, Bailey, del Barrio)

A bright, tropical feel accompanies the aptly-named 'Sparkle'. Bailey takes the lead vocal, and the broken drum feel helps the track stand out. Bailey hangs over the turning chord sequence while the guitars call and respond. The chorus arrives soon enough, and the groove switches to a straight four. The horns answer Bailey's vocal parts with vigour.

A brief horn-led section begins after the second chorus before Bailey sends the track over the top with his stellar vocal prowess. Not the group's most-discussed track, 'Sparkle' qualifies as a hidden gem in the EW&F catalogue.

'Back On The Road' (White, McKay)

Strangely for a track written by Maurice and Al, 'Back On The Road' features a lot of Steve Lukather, who was fresh off recording Boz Scaggs' *Middle Man* album. Steve begins the track on his own, riffing with a distorted, chorus-soaked rock tone for a solid 10 seconds. He shoots off a rapid descending dive-bomb, the band coming in with a thumping rhythm while Lukather plays some hot licks.

The lyric is a paean to touring and the endless highways a superstar band traverses. Maurice takes the lead vocal, the verse melody is simple but effective. Bailey pops up for the chorus, and the track rolls along nicely like one of the tour buses the group would've used at the time. Lukather takes a superb, tasteful solo, playing like the seasoned pro he was by this point. The chorus repeats, with more guitar licks in the fade-out.

'Back On The Road' was a single in the UK, where it reached 63.

'Song In My Heart' (White, Russell, Glenn)

This up-tempo cut with a disco feel wouldn't sound out of place on the 1979 hit Michael Jackson album *Off The Wall,* which in turn had a similar vibe. Again, Verdine's bass is blended with synth to create weight with the drums, and guitar doubles the verse bass line before the chorus brings a celebratory feel.

Multi-layered vocals fill the section before the chords jump upwards back to the verse. A key change in the second and final chorus raises the feeling before quickly ducking back down to the original key.

'You Went Away' (Bailey, Vannelli)

The only track without Maurice's writing input was penned by Bailey with Ross Vannelli – brother of Canadian superstar Gino Vannelli (hot off the success of his album *Brother to Brother*). Guitarist Steve Lukather returns, playing a bluesy intro lick. Bailey sounds heartbroken as he tells of a love gone bad. 'How can you explain that we're apart/When all we've known is being together'. The song slowly builds towards the chorus, complete with a key change and a smooth rhythm bursting through. The bass pushes the track along, and after the mountainous chorus peak, verse two drops back to a romantic groove.

Lukather takes a heartfelt solo after the second chorus before Bailey and the sweeping strings return. Bailey's vocal ad-libs over the outro are monstrous, eventually disappearing in a vortex of reverb, only for Lukather to take over with blistering runs over the fade-out.

'And Love Goes On' (White, White, Dunn, Foster)

The chorused piano of the intro recalls The Doobie Brothers' 1979 hit 'What A Fool Believes'. Horns punctuate the first beat of every bar, before a rising note chain leads to the verse. Maurice begins it with confidence, attacking the notes, before pivoting to the chorus' longer, sustained lines. The sections repeat, before the bridge cycles through a four-chord pattern, which then repeats a minor third above. The feel makes it nearly impossible for the listener to be unhappy, and the positive vibes make this an underrated EW&F cut.

'Sailaway' (White, Bailey, del Barrio, Seeman)

'Sailaway' provides a breather in the album sequencing – an easy-listening waltz that sees Bailey live out any big-band aspirations he may have had. He and Maurice wrote the song with Eddie del Barrio, and Roxanne Seeman, who later worked with Phil Collins, Chaka Khan and The Sisters of Mercy. Two distinct vocal melodies manage to form above the chords, the simplicity washing over the listener as the track lives up to its title. The dynamics rise considerably before falling back down in cinematic fashion. Verdine sneaks some bass pops into the track, and eventually, it returns to the beginning – almost roller-coaster-like – before Rhamlee Michael Davis takes a relaxed flugelhorn solo. The parts repeat, there's another solo from Davis, and Bailey performs jazz-like intervals, bringing the track to a close with class – it eventually dissolves on a slightly ominous chord.

'Take It To The Sky' (White, Dunn, Glenn)

This begins with a lush guitar intro. Maurice is given the main vocal, and settles into a nice half-time groove which at times is reminiscent of the group's earlier work. They pick up for the chorus, Dunn's line moving back and forth underneath the vocal hook. The bridge chord progression also recalls other tracks by the group – perhaps a little too much: in particular, 'That's The Way Of The World'. A McKay solo is followed by a few choruses until the end.

'Win Or Lose' (Hancock, Peters)

This music was written by Jerry Peters (who wrote 'Burnin' Bush' on *Spirit*), with lyrics by Jean Hancock (sister of jazz pianist Herbie) – who died tragically in a plane crash a few years later. Strings add tension behind the catchy vocal hook. Synth and bass collide, skanking guitars filling up the bars as the Bailey-led verse begins. The beginning hook returns for the chorus, with Bailey adding vocal harmonies. The string arrangement by Tom Tom 84 really sweetened the track, bringing a cinematic element.

'Win Or Lose' deserves more attention than it received, and would've made a great single.

'Share Your Love' (White, Glenn)
This up-tempo track has vocals scattered along the intro synth line before the stomping verse begins. Bailey joins for a powerful chorus as he bounces staccato lines around with Maurice, providing a call-and-response melody with the trumpet in verse two. A horn-filled bridge provides a break before the final chorus repeats begin, with more bebop style vocal lines scattered throughout as the track fades away.

It's not the album's lowest point, but certainly isn't its highest. Though there's nothing technically wrong, a complacency creeps through.

'In Time' (White, Matza, McCrary)
Fender Rhodes and acoustic piano play the intro before the band begins, punctuated by a pounding floor tom. The rhythm is a mid-tempo thump with a slightly odd bass riff. The horns and drums are tight, and Maurice handles the lead, his double-tracked vocal with just enough reverb to lend some atmosphere. The chorus continues with the same riff, Bailey bringing in the great hook, 'In time, you will know it in time'. The bridge is filled with majestic chord changes, with a straight four bringing respite from the relentless groove. Bailey glides through the chord changes until the groove reappears. After another verse and chorus, the horns go through a series of modulating chord changes out of the blue. 'In Time' fades on the riff it has so-firmly established.

'Faces' (White, White, Dunn, Bailey)
The complex introduction is a piece of fusion with an almost big-band vibe. What comes next may be slightly unexpected, as the group brings in a fast percussion-filled samba recalling the work of Weather Report. Verdine holds down the rhythm, scratchy guitar filling in the spaces. 'Many faces listen to the sound/Different places span the globe around', Maurice and Philip intone, proposing a message of worldly togetherness. Graham takes a fuzz solo as Dunn plays around underneath. Complex changes take us to a written jazz-head-style section between trumpet and Fender Rhodes, followed by a brilliant Dunn piano solo, interacting with the group spontaneously. Michael Harris takes an excellent brief solo, before the trumpet and Rhodes repeat their lines from before, the string section raising the track to fever pitch. Woolfolk takes a typically excellent solo, slowly raising the intensity before the group fires off some amazing accents, in between which the string section plays incredibly fast and complex lines to bring the track to a close. A short, gospel pipe organ interlude finishes up the album.

Raise! (1981)

Personnel:
Maurice White: vocals, drums, kalimba
Verdine White: bass, vocals
Ralph Johnson: drums, percussion
Philip Bailey: vocals, percussion
Roland Bautista, Johnny Graham: guitar
Larry Dunn: piano, synthesizer, programming
Fred White: drums
Andrew Woolfolk: tenor saxophone
Louis Satterfield: trombone
Michael Harris: trumpet
Don Myrick: alto, tenor and baritone saxophone
Rhamlee Michael Davis: trumpet, flugelhorn
Additional Musicians:
Tom Saviano: saxophone
Bill Reichenbach, Charles Loper, Dick Hyde, George Bohanon, Lew McRear: trombone
Chuck Findley, Gary Grant, Jerry Hey, Larry G. Hall: trumpet
Assa Dori, James Getzoff: concertmaster
Billy Meyers, David Foster, Wayne Vaughn: keyboards
Michael Boddicker: synthersizer, vocoder
Beloyd Taylor: additional guitar
Ms. Pluto: additional vocals
Producers: Maurice White, Larry Dunn
Engineers: Ron Pendragon, Ken Fowler, Mick Guzauski, Tom Perry, Stephen McManus
Studios: ARC Studios, Sunset Sound, Los Angeles, CA
Mastering: Mike Reese at The Mastering Lab
Release date: 14 November 1981
Chart positions: US: 5, 1 (Soul), UK: 11
Running time: 38:28

After *Faces* failed to yield any hits, Maurice and the group were under more pressure than ever to come up with the goods. As Maurice began to compile songs for the new album, he often wrote with Bernard 'Beloyd' Taylor, who had co-wrote 'Getaway' on *Spirit*. Maurice told him he was searching for simpler songs to have a more electronic feel, falling in line with the sounds of the day. Beloyd came back with 'Lady Sun' and 'You Are A Winner', and also co-wrote 'The Changing Times'. Maurice later recalled these songs setting the tone for the album, but was still casting the song net wide open, and another songwriter caught his ear. Wayne Vaughn was married to The Emotions' Wanda Hutchinson: another ARC mainstay. Vaughn's writing style meshed well with Maurice', and they came up with 'My Love', 'Wanna

Be With You', and the last track recorded for the project – 'Let's Groove' – which eventually bumped 'You Are A Winner' as the album's first single.

Musician changes also took place. Roland Bautista was back as a core band member with his rocking guitar style, while again scores of session musicians were hired. Amongst these the horn trio of Jerry Hey, Chuck Findley and Bill Reichenbach got more of the sessions than before, leaving a growing resentment from The Phenix Horns. Also, studio wizard George Massenburg was absent.

The resulting album *Raise!* again used artist Shusei Nagaoka to reflect Maurice's vision for the album cover, which this time merged the ancient with futurism. The tour was the biggest yet, costing over $60,000 a night and employing a crew of 60 with 14 trailers of gear. But what no one saw coming (besides perhaps the band themselves possibly) was how 'Let's Groove' would become such a hit. Climbing to 3 in the US and UK, and reaching the top 10 in numerous countries, 'Let's Groove' put EW&F back on the map. Also, 'Wanna Be With You' won a Grammy for Best R&B Vocal Performance by a Duo or Group: further cementing the album's success.

But hitting the top of the charts again, came at a price, as serious cracks started to show in the group. Fred White developed a serious drug problem, and the time off Maurice granted him led to accusations of nepotism. Philip Bailey wrote in *Shining Star*: 'I basically became just a session singer. Maurice and I would lay down our background vocals. Bang! Done! That was the vibe through those records. Although we won another Grammy award – Best R&B Vocal Performance by a Duo or Group – for 'Wanna Be With You' from *Raise!*, our momentum had stalled'.

The issues with The Phenix Horns would also come to a head on the tour – Louis Satterfield and Don Myrick cornering Maurice before a show at the L.A. Forum, demanding more money for their services, or they wouldn't turn up onstage. This was the last straw for Maurice, who didn't use them on record again. But the Phenix Horns played on plenty more records by other artists, most notably Phil Collins and Genesis.

'Let's Groove' (White, Vaughn)
Maurice said of the hit 'Let's Groove': 'The Multiple hooks over that one great groove gave the song an exciting-yet-simple approach. The horns are held back until the bridge, which added a 1940s big-band swing sound. Bill Meyers' horn arrangement turned up the joyous vibe, which is why I think the song feels so good'.

The track also came with a promotional film clip directed by Michael Schultz (the man behind the movie *Car Wash* and television show *Starsky & Hutch*, who later worked with artists as diverse as Queen Latifah, Extreme, L7 and NWA). His vision captured the essence of EW&F, using blue-screen technology to project the group into outer space, immaculate costumes and all. The multicoloured trails behind the group members became iconic.

Though they'd filmed promos for 'Serpentine Fire', 'September', 'Boogie Wonderland' and 'Let Me Talk', getting them played was terribly limited before MTV. Unfortunately, 'Let's Groove' didn't get played either – not because MTV didn't exist, but because (as Maurice mentioned in his autobiography) 'The network was unapologetically racist. Rick James and Earth, Wind & Fire had two of the biggest records in the country. Despite our outcry, MTV refused to play either video'. But one channel that *did* pick up the video was the burgeoning Black Entertainment Television, and 'Let's Groove' was the first track to be played on their new show *Video Soul*.

The track begins with kick drum, and two voices through a vocoder – one octave occupying the usual sonic territory of the bass. Celebratory horns and chimes swirl around, announcing that something special is about to occur. In the chorus, Philip Bailey and Ms. Pluto (aka The Emotions' Wanda Hutchinson) appear with one of the most catchy vocal lines ever.

So far, all the melodies have occurred over the same chord progression, but the bridge moves to a new, dramatic set of chords, ending with accents on the line 'boogie on down'. Another chorus is followed by an instrumental section highlighting the horn section before the chorus is milked for all it's worth.

'Let's Groove' was the album's most successful single, reaching 3 in the US and UK.

'Lady Sun' (Taylor)

This has a slightly more rock feel, the heavy guitar sitting just underneath the horn lines, and synthesizers punctuate the track. Bailey and White sing together, before Maurice takes the verse. The lyric uses weather as a metaphor for love. The slightly nasal vocal attack recalls later 1980s electro-funk hits, and a brief pre-chorus gives way to the chorus' call-and-response between Maurice and the backing vocals. The post-chorus horn-and-vocal interplay is a track highlight. Horns punctuate the next verse, and the guitar bumps up the funk; the post-chorus section extends to the end.

'Lady Sun' is a great funk track, and finds the band adjusting their sound away from disco, though sitting in the shadow of 'Let's Groove' doesn't do it any favours.

'My Love' (White, Vaughn)

This track exudes the confident, brooding strut of the quiet-storm genre (which was named from the Smokey Robinson track) – adopted by artists like Marvin Gaye and Sade, and known for its romantic, adult grooves. The interplay between Maurice and the backing vocals here is something to behold, the rhythm anticipating the end of every two-bar pattern. The pre-chorus adds Bailey and Hutchinson, who eventually takes the lead, dropping back down to the verse. The horns join for the following sections, sexy sax adding to the mood.

'Evolution Orange' (White, Foster, O'Byrne)

This was co-written with Nan O'Byrne, who later worked with The Pointer Sisters and Bonnie Raitt. A promising four-on-the-floor features a fast guitar line, percussion, squelchy synth and the horn section until the groove breaks down under a blazing string-section run and the verse is established. Bailey works the lead vocal, sounding slightly rough around the edges. The pre-chorus adopts a more punctuated style, followed by a chorus that never quite feels like a payoff for the excitement of the intro. Verse two's vocal effects don't quite gel with the track, his vocal loud and alone feeling in the mix. 'Evolution Orange' seems to usher in elements that didn't work so well over the coming releases, and Bailey came to despise the track.

'Kalimba Tree' (White, White, Hey)

A futuristic, swirling synth note opens side two. It's a brief interlude with filtered music that's actually part of the intro to the next track.

'You Are A Winner' (Taylor)

A stuttering bass-synth riff leans against the rhythm in Beloyd Taylor's next album contribution. The vocals intone a repeating three-note-chord 'cha cha cha cha' hook until Maurice begins the first verse with a melody that scales to the top of his register. Interesting chord changes lead to the chorus, after which Bautista's distorted guitar bursts onto the scene, dominating the mix with power chords.

'You Are A Winner' is a well-played, well-produced slice of funk, though – aside from the modern technology – nothing is said here that hadn't already been said by the group previously.

'I've Had Enough' (Bailey, Russell, Phillinganes)

The second single happens to be the album's other highlight, though it only charted in the UK, where it reached 29. The co-writers were singer-songwriter Brenda Russell and keyboard player Greg Phillinganes.

Phillinganes had been discovered by Stevie Wonder, and played in his backing group, Wonderlove, before hitting big with his work on The Jacksons' hit albums *Victory* and *Triumph*. This led to a huge role on Michael Jackson's *Thriller* album.

Opening with a fade-in that turns into group-accentuated horn stabs, a percussion-filled groove leads to Bailey's excellent verse performance. The melody soars over the Latin-jazz chord vamp before descending into the brief pre-chorus. The chorus contains a truly memorable melody. Maurice takes the octave down from Bailey to thicken up the vocals before heading to an instrumental break.

Though not a high-charting single, the serene chorus is worth the price of admission alone.

'Wanna Be With You' (White, Vaughn)

This lurching shuffle climbed to 51 in the US, and is evidence of the quality disparity between the album tracks and the singles. Though perhaps not as catchy as 'Let's Groove' or 'I've Had Enough', 'Wanna Be With You' remains captivating. The slow rhythm appears after a short Fender Rhodes and acoustic piano intro. Bailey and Maurice launch a repetitive 'Wanna be, wanna be, wanna be, be with her' chant, as silky horns bring instrumental depth. Maurice sings lead for the verse, beginning as a whisper before growing in power. This is followed by the chorus, Wanda Hutchinson again leaving her mark with a high, breathy vocal. The end of the second chorus brings a brief key modulation and a bridge. At the end, the music is filtered down to a telephone frequency. A great groove helps the track, despite its lack of chart success.

'The Changing Times' (Taylor, Vaughan, White)

A rock guitar riff ushers in an up-tempo rhythm, complete with complex dual synthesizer lines from Dunn. Maurice and Philip bring in the 'bup be bup be ba' vocal line as the band bounces back and forth beneath them. Guitar power chords soon enter, as Maurice and Bailey split verse one between them. The pre-chorus has a fusion-like chord sequence, before the unmemorable chorus of 'Space on the strife/Fix up your life' finds the song hitting a snag. Bautista's ending solo is a slight step down from the guitar work of Steve Lukather – his nimble, graceful and tasty playing replaced with occasionally-off-sounding blues bends.

It's a disappointing end to the album from a track that starts off promisingly. Despite the hit presence of 'Let's Groove' and the outside songwriters called in, the dip in track quality is noticeable and hard to ignore, and the resulting splinters in the lineup would soon be felt.

Powerlight (1983)

Personnel:
Maurice White: vocals, drums, kalimba, percussion
Verdine White: bass, vocals
Ralph Johnson, Philip Bailey: vocals, percussion
Roland Bautista, Johnny Graham: guitar
Larry Dunn: synthesizer, programming
Fred White: drums
Andrew Woolfolk: tenor saxophone
Louis Satterfield: trombone
Michael Harris: trumpet
Don Myrick: alto, tenor and baritone saxophone
Rhamlee Michael Davis: trumpet, flugelhorn
Additional Musicians:
Chuck Findley, Gary Grant: trumpet
Bill Reichenbach, Charles Lopez, George Bohanon, Lew McCreary: trombone
Steve Lukather, Beloyd Taylor: guitar
Eddie del Barrio, Rick Kelly, Skip Scarborough, Wayne Vaughn: keyboards
Robert Greenidge: steel drums
Zakir Hussein: tabla
Producer: Maurice White
Engineers: Mick Guzauski, Tom Perry, Robert Spano, Steve Crimmel
Studios: The Complex, Ocean Way, Los Angeles, CA
Mixing: Mick Guzauski
Mastering: Bernie Grundman at A&M
Release date: 3 February 1983
Chart positions: US: 12, 4 (R&B), UK: 22
Running time: 41:13

The 18 months between *Raise!* and *Powerlight* saw some interesting developments for EW&F, and significant changes in pop culture. 1982 saw the release of Michael Jackson's seminal (and heavily EW&F-influenced) *Thriller*, which was produced by Maurice's old friend Quincy Jones, and dominated the airwaves throughout 1983. Prince had sculpted funk into his own vision – the Minneapolis sound – leading the way for his protege acts like The Time, and super-producers in-waiting Jimmy Jam and Terry Lewis. Could EW&F still hang with the younger musicians that adored them?

Though the band members were still around, the situation was slowly fragmenting. Bailey was busy working on his debut solo album *Continuation* with producer George Duke: released just months after *Powerlight*. Meanwhile, ARC was feeling the strain of Maurice's missing-in-action ownership style, and was to close down not long after. He'd always considered himself to be a musician fulfilling a businessman's role, and that idea had turned into a self-fulfilling prophecy – given his track record with finances he would have clearly benefited from outside help. Despite this, the Complex Studio was increasingly in demand by high-profile artists.

For this album, Maurice turned largely to the same songwriters as last time. There are studio musicians galore, and the six keyboard players (not including Dunn) fill the tracks with early-1980s synth sounds. EW&F had slowly transformed into followers, instead of leaders. *Powerlight* only reached 12 in the US and 22 in the UK, though one single – the great 'Fall in Love With Me' – reached 17 in the US. The album is not without its merit, but is generally remembered as something of a disappointment.

'Fall In Love With Me' (White, Vaughn, Vaughn)

Powerlight opens with its best-known cut. Synth chords move in an upward motion, and we hear the same programming technique Dunn had employed on the *Faces* track 'Let Me Talk' – sounding a little too similar to get the track/album off to an exciting, fresh start. Then it's into foot stomping funk territory with some futuristic synth. Verdine only pops on bass – above synth bass – but his playing adds a human element (along with the guitar) to the ice-cold drum machine beat.

Maurice is right up front for the verse. Bailey arrives in a big way with 'Baby, you know' highlighted by the group. The vocal hook is irresistible, rising and falling like a mountain range. Bailey sings the lead while Maurice responds in the background. The track eventually drops down to the bass, drums and percussion groove, before Steve Lukather takes a smouldering solo – originally cut from pressings (along with the breakdown), making the track nearly a full minute and a half shorter.

'Spread Your Love' (White, Taylor, Lawrence)

Layered vocals sing 'Spread your love around' several times before the track reveals its dance-floor thump. Maurice is doubled up by a vocoder up an octave for the verse. The chorus continues over the static-chord groove. The second verse continues with the vocoder before some impressive vocal layering, after which the chorus repeats. Later, the main rhythm returns with a surprising steel-drum solo.

The track became the album's third single, hitting 57 R&B in the US. Maurice and Beloyd co-wrote it with Rhett Lawrence, who went on to work with Whitney Houston and Paula Abdul, and wrote Mariah Carey's first hit 'Vision Of Love'.

Pleasing enough, 'Spread Your Love' suffers from the lack of a memorable chorus, though it has some interesting moments.

'Side By Side' (White, Vaughn, Vaughn)

Soft, gentle electric piano opens 'Side By Side', as Maurice begins his first verse, giving the listener the false sense that a ballad may be about to occur. But what follows is a slice of funky R&B, with plenty of Wanda Hutchinson's exquisite, warm vocals. The Phenix Horns fill up the track, and though they'd had something of a falling out, Maurice still hired them on the sessions, along with other brass players.

Maurice takes the lead again for the bridge, and another steel-drum solo takes place. Choruses repeat, the vocals disappearing for a time before more steel-drum soloing. Before the next track begins, some excellent tabla-playing by Ustad Zakir Hussain is heard. Disappointingly, the single – the album's second – only reached 76 in the US.

'Straight From The Heart' (Bailey, del Barrio, Seeman, Washington)
This is Philip Bailey's only songwriting contribution to the album. Co-writer bassist Freddie Washington – who'd worked with artists like Herbie Hancock, Boz Scaggs and Herb Alpert – was coming off a co-write of Patrice Rushen's hit 'Forget Me Nots'. But 'Straight From The Heart' takes a completely different route, with sweet strings arranged by Eddie del Barrio's brother George del Barrio. Bailey gives a great performance. The predictable verse is thrown out for a chorus with unexpected chord changes. The bridge contains some great vocals, and a nifty key change extends to the final chorus, giving Bailey more room for vocal licks in the fade. Not the band's most memorable ballad, it's devoid of excitement, with nothing that puts it over the edge.

'The Speed Of Love' (White, Vaughn, Haynes)
Side two begins with big, whirling horns and tom fills, before a bass-synth-driven groove starts with a swinging drum groove. Written by Maurice with Wayne Vaughn and lyricist Tony Haynes (who would go on to work with Robert Palmer and Bobby Brown). The melody travels through the jazz changes, keeping low before busting out towards the end of the section, landing on a crescendo that plays into the chorus. The next section may be the most interesting, Maurice keeping the vocal smooth, before Philip and Wanda join for 'at the speed of love', the last word climbing higher and higher thanks to the tape vari-speed effect applied.

'Freedom Of Choice' (White, Taylor, Lawrence)
This track has a fast bass-synth groove. Bautista's guitar licks take the lead, before Bailey begins the verse. The lyric is hostile, giving an angry-on-the-dance-floor feel, and it's all the better for it.

You gave your vote to pass the law
Do you want to take it back?
All the bad news we read about today
Is because our system's on the rack
Can you make your dreams straight reality?
Can you dig the prime interest rates?
Do you think you'd meet hospitality
If you went to the White House by mistake?

The vocal overdubs sound like a group of protesters with an unusually good sense of harmony. Bursting rock-guitar power chords take over in the bridge, dropping away momentarily for Dunn's lightning-fast synth runs and Bautista's clean, bluesy licks.

One of this album's better cuts, 'Freedom of Choice' has a memorable chorus, and the angry vibe makes for interesting listening.

'Something Special' (White, Vaughn)

Sparkling, sequenced synth lines hover in the air, beginning 'Something Special' with a mystical tone. The half-time shuffle feel locks in with vamping piano chords, while Verdine pops the bass with nasty intentions. The track recalls pre-synth EW&F, despite the intro synth sequencing. Maurice's vocal sits like a jewel between the backing vocals, before group accents begin the chorus. Afterwards, they take a big-band turn, the horns playing a swinging melody as distorted guitar weaves around them. Maurice scats towards the end, reminding the listener of his strong jazz background.

'Hearts To Heart' (White, Taylor, Lawrence)

After intro vocals and guitar, a chugging funk riff begins over a staccato synth-bass part. The verse is full of inspirational lines, Maurice telling the listener that if they 'feel out of shape and you need to communicate/Get up, explore/Tune in and you can't ignore'. The pre-chorus is full of rising gospel vocals, before a slightly strange chorus zaps the energy away momentarily. The sliding bass notes are interesting but, unfortunately, result in the groove bottoming out. Largely forgettable, 'Hearts To Heart' never quite takes flight.

'Miracles' (White, del Barrio, Lind, D'Astugues)

This piano-driven ballad has theatrical undertones. Co-writer Mary D'Astugues later worked closely with Cher on her *Heart of Stone* album. If one word could be used to sum up this track, it would have to be 'epic'. The huge scope evokes endless desert landscapes. But first, it begins with interesting piano chords (doubled with Fender Rhodes) and Maurice singing:

Let's put the day aside
Let peaceful thoughts arise
May your dreams be sweet tonight
With kisses on your cheek
And wings upon your feet

Bailey joins in the pre-chorus, moving through complex intervals in an impressive display. The chords already lend themselves to a visual component but fully blossom when later augmented by band and horns. The closing choruses are a marvel to behold. The reoccurring bar of 7/8 in is arranging genius, propelling the chorus onwards.

Electric Universe (1983)

Personnel:
Maurice White: vocals, drums, kalimba
Verdine White: bass
Ralph Johnson: percussion
Philip Bailey: vocals
Roland Bautista: guitar
Larry Dunn: synthesizer, piano, programming
Fred White: drums, percussion
Andrew Woolfolk: tenor saxophone
Additional Musicians:
David Foster, Michael Colombier, Wayne Vaughn: keyboards
Brian Fairweather, Martin Page, Robbie Buchanon: synthersizer programming
Producer: Maurice White
Engineer: Mick Guzauski
Studios: The Complex, Ocean Way, Los Angeles, CA
Mixing: George Massenburg
Mastering: Bernie Grundman at A&M Studios
Release date: 4 November 1983
Chart positions: US: 40, US soul: 8, UK: 18 (Blues & Soul)
Running time: 36:21

The disappointing sales of *Powerlight* sent the group scrambling in an attempt to climb back to the top and the achievements of 'Let's Groove'. Before recording for the new album began, the group appeared on the soundtrack of the animated movie *Rock & Rule*. Their contribution 'Dance, Dance, Dance' (no relation to the Chic classic), was a four-on-the-floor thumper and a highlight of the largely-forgotten cult movie.

Maurice continued to seek inspiration in the new electronic sounds of younger acts – growing tired of the sound EW&F had cultivated over the years. He noted in his autobiography:

> By the fall of 1983, I was getting bored with R&B. Records like 'She Blinded Me With Science' by Thomas Dolby, 'Owner Of A Lonely Heart' by Yes and 'I Can't Go For That' by Hall and Oates were turning me on. All songs had a European flavour – pared-down, electronic and yet very song-driven. This was the direction I felt Earth, Wind & Fire should go.

Longtime EW&F guitarist Johnny Graham left the group after *Powerlight*. Bob Cavallo introduced Maurice to a pair of British songwriters, whom he believed held the key to transitioning to the new style he envisioned. Martin Page and Brian Fairweather (bass and guitar, respectively) led British synthpop group Q-Feel, whose song 'Dancing In Heaven (Orbital Be-Bop)' had been an entrant in the 1982 Eurovision Song Contest. Maurice and the two songwriters had a mutual fascination with UFOs, so he decided to work with them on what became *Electric Universe*. The sci-fi interest bled into the album's lyric themes (a distrust of technology – while (ironically) using the latest in music tech to make the statements) and artwork.

Multiple session musicians were again used, and engineer George Massenburg returned. Reviews mostly praised the group for their new style, though the album came nowhere near the success Maurice wanted – instead seeming to ring the death knell for the band's time at the top. The album's singles barely made a dent – 'Magnetic' climbing the highest (57 in the US) – maybe thanks to its high-budget sci-fi video clip.

By 1984, the writing was on the wall, and Maurice called a band meeting at The Complex. He was placing the group on hiatus, and beginning work on a solo album. He told *The Times*' Dennis Hunt in 1986: 'The band is on hiatus. We worked together for over 12 years. It's just time to do things on our own. I don't want to be forced to do an album because of a contractual obligation. We'll probably do something together again, but I don't know when'. The group's bitterness was evident in interviews – Bailey later telling Dennis Hunt (while doing the rounds for Bailey's 1984 solo album *Chinese Wall*) when asked when the hiatus would end: 'I don't know. Go ask Maurice. If anybody knows, he does'. Not all EW&F members stay in the industry – Ralph Johnson moved on to more normal pursuits (before later rejoining the band), and recalled to CBS News: 'When somebody kind of pulls that rug out, now you've gotta rethink your whole program. I called a friend of mine who had a construction company. I went down and helped him install fire sprinklers. And then later on, I went to work at Federated Stereo, selling stereos, which I was very comfortable with'. Pull the rug out, indeed. The glorious first run of Earth, Wind & Fire had come to an end after producing more hits than a Tyson fight.

'Magnetic' (Page)

The influence of Page and Fairweather is felt strongly in the opening track (and first single) 'Magnetic'. An electro rhythm comes in with a dive-bombing rock guitar. Vocals are the only thing stopping the track (and album) from heading into full robot territory. Lines like 'A strange kind of light/The tempo takes me and the circuit excites', reflect the album's futuristic theme. The chorus warns us that 'Rhythm of a dangerous dance' will 'Suck you in twice as fast'.

In the bridge, Maurice says he will be making 'contact' – a buzzword for those inclined to look into extraterrestrial happenings. Verdine's slapping and popping bass in the next section provides a natural touch. A new hook arrives for the outro – 'Step in the light tonight/Make the sparks ignite' – and the song is out. The synths and programmed drums now date the album, though it could be seen as holding some retro charm.

The single 'Magnetic' reached a disappointing 57 in the US, but 10 on the R&B chart.

'Touch' (White, Lind)

The third single has a mid-tempo groove, given feel by Verdine's bass line. Booming toms beckon the verse, and Maurice uses an intimate vocal tone to get the emotion across. Rising backing vocals signal the pre-chorus before the chorus' catchy hook, striking synth and whip-cracking drums. Bailey's deadpan delivery of 'Touch, touch' is well in line with other pop of the day, and the group pivot to a turnaround at the end of the chorus.

'Touch' missed the US Hot 100 but reached 23 R&B and 36 Adult Contemporary.

'Moonwalk' (Porter, O'Connor)

If EW&F had been one of Michael Jackson's major influences, perhaps their song title 'Moonwalk' was a tip of the hat to the king of pop, considering *Electric Universe* was released mere months after Jackson wowed the world with his new 'moonwalk' dance move at the Motown 25th Anniversary concert in May 1983. Musically though, the track doesn't quite live up to Jackson's output at the time. The rhythm and coldness is slightly tempered by Maurice's vocal, but the production is quite heavy-handed. The chorus is more inspired than the verse, with Wanda Vaughn and Pamela Hutchinson taking the lead for the melody's odd intervals, making for intriguing listening.

Eventually, 'Moonwalk' became the album's fourth single, hitting 67 on the soul chart.

'Could It Be Right' (White, Willis, Foster)

The album's first ballad closes side one, and again chases the Adult Contemporary market, feeling like a precursor to the animated Disney movies of the 1990s. A short, sweet introduction gives way to the verse, simply featuring Maurice with electric piano. Predictably, the drum groove picks up from the second verse onwards, as does Verdine, whose bass-playing is a track highlight.

It's a nice enough, inoffensive ballad but lacks the emotional depth of the group's earlier ballad work.

'Spirit Of A New World' (White, Page, Foster, Fairweather)

Side two's first track wouldn't sound out of place in a *Rocky* movie. Maurice gives the verse his all over the fast straight-four rhythm – the kick and snare programmed through a Simmons electric kit. The pre-chorus' pronounced rock vibe continues into the chorus.

Step into the dance
We step into the dance of life
Let the rhythm take a chance
We can make the spirit rise

A key change and a big rock riff define the bridge, hectic keyboards zooming around. A descending guitar line interrupts the next chorus, followed by a stream of sparkling synth notes. After a sax solo backed with burning guitars and ethereal vocal harmonies, a final chorus ends the song abruptly.

'Sweet Sassy Lady' (White, Vaughn, Hutchinson, Vaughn)
This begins with a lazy synth riff over a straight-ahead rhythm. Guitar synth drives over the top, adding an interesting tonal touch. Maurice's voice echoes back at him in the verses, panning across the stereo spectrum with subtle phaser for extra sci-fi style. The pre-chorus chord changes are surprisingly bluesy, before the chorus emits its poppy hook. The bridge is stripped back, and soon eschewed for the full groove with new chords and lyrics. Some rather-uneventful chorus turns see the track fade out. It has some great moments but doesn't particularly stand out in the group's canon.

'We're Living In Our Own Time' (White, Willis, Colombier)
The album's second ballad was co-written with renowned film-score composer Michel Colombier. Bailey is found at his most gentle and bombastic at different points. A pulsing synthetic wash adds a different dimension to a track that's otherwise par for the course. Despite great musicianship, this track is too cliched to be anything memorable on its own terms.

'Electric Nation' (White, Page, Fairweather)
EW&F fans didn't realise this would be the last they'd be hearing of the group for quite some time. The album's second single didn't chart, and didn't quite live up to even the medium-level bar set by 'Magnetic'. What could well be just another rock guitar riff in another group's hands, anchors the track. Technology again dominates the lyric.

We're living by computer
The sound is rushing through ya
Believe in what your eyes see
Your in touch with the energy

The vocal harmonies that tie the bridge to the final chorus show top-notch arranging skills. An instrumental section follows, featuring Maurice scatting. Chorused guitar leads the group to the fade – closing the album, and an era.

Touch The World (1987)

Personnel:
Maurice White: vocals, drums, vocoder, kalimba
Ralph Johnson: percussion
Philip Bailey: vocals
Sheldon Reynolds: guitar
Andrew Woolfolk: tenor saxophone
Additional Musicians:
Skylark: drum programming, synthersizer programming, backing vocals ('System of Survival')
Rhett Lawrence: drum programming, synthersizer programming
Paul Jackson, Ray Fuller: guitar
Nathan East: bass
Jeff Porcaro, Ricky Lawson: drums
Jeanette Williams, Wayne Vaughn: backing vocals
Producers: Maurice White, with Preston Glass ('System Of Survival') and Bill Meyers ('New Horizons')
Engineers: Tom Lord-Alge, David Rideau
Mixing: George Massenburg
Studios: Studio Ultimo, Amigo Studios, Studio D, Different Fur, Soundcastle, California
Mastering: George Marino at Sterling Sound
Release date: 17 November 1987
Chart positions: US: 33, US soul: 3, UK: 16 (Blues & Soul)
Running time: 42:40

Touch The World was the beginning of a new chapter in the group's career. In the years since *Electric Universe,* Maurice had produced other artists (notably Neil Diamond), and released an eponymous solo album that unfortunately didn't fare well critically or commercially. Philip Bailey had released his *Chinese Wall* album, sending him into megastar territory, thanks in particular to his hit duet with Phil Collins: 'Easy Lover'. The other group members stayed in close orbit with each other. Larry Dunn and Verdine White co-produced the 1983 Level 42 album *Standing In The Light,* on which Andrew Woolfolk also appeared. Dunn and Bautista played on Morris Day's album away from The Time: *Color of Success.* Despite Bailey having the most success away from EW&F, it was his idea to get the band back together. In *Shining Star,* he recalled the impact his stardom had on his dealings with Maurice:

My newfound success had put me on a different bargaining level. *Chinese Wall* had been certified Gold in the United States in 1985, while Maurice's long-awaited self-titled solo debut on Columbia barely cracked 200,000 copies that same year. My solo success forced Maurice to deal with me as an equal, just as Phil Collins had treated me as an equal and not as a little brother.

At first resistant to the idea of regrouping, Maurice eventually agreed, mainly to help get him out of a financial bind. The problem was he hadn't spoken to Verdine in months after the two had a disagreement over property. Feelers were sent out to McKay and Dunn, but neither wanted any involvement. The golden lineup would not be returning. Ralph Johnson and Andrew Woolfolk *were* happy to jump aboard for the ride, and Maurice asked former Commodores guitarist Sheldon Reynolds to join. A new horn section was also needed, so Maurice formed The Earth, Wind & Fire horns – Gary Bias on sax, Raymond Lee Brown on trumpet, and Reggie Young on flugelhorn and trombone. A host of studio musicians were brought in – notably Nathan East on bass, The Yellowjackets' Ricky Lawson (drums) and Marc Russo (saxophone), Toto drummer Jeff Porcaro, Michael Jackson guitarist Paul Jackson Jr. and the legendary George Duke on keyboards.

Touch the World was released to positive reviews, and though it didn't set the charts alight, it reached a respectable 33 in the US. Verdine and Maurice made up for the tour, which introduced newcomers Vance Taylor (keyboards) and Sonny Emory (drums). Unfortunately, the tour was a commercial failure, taking the group to the financial brink and ensuring the necessity to continue to recoup their losses. Bailey later recalled the situation in *Shining Star*:

It was a very dark and humbling experience. While we had a few good box offices in New York, Chicago and Los Angeles, in the rest of the country, we fared pretty poorly. The last straw came when we played a very bizarre show in Japan. It was a gig that took place during the half-time of an auto race. The promoters set up a giant stage in the centre of the racetrack, where we were to perform. The crowd hadn't come to hear music, and the concert was a disaster. We were merely a sideshow in some out-of-the-way city. Afterward on the way to the airport, Maurice and I solemnly looked at each other, crestfallen. 'You know what?', Maurice said to me – 'I'd rather leave the legacy behind and let it be what it's gonna be, because this is not it'. We both agreed.

'System Of Survival' (Skylark)

Written by Skylark and produced by Preston Glass, 'System Of Survival' updates the EW&F sound. Glass began his career alongside famed Philadelphia producer Thom Bell, and by the late-1980s had earned a reputation for his smooth adult-contemporary jazz production with artists like Kenny G and George Benson.

The track begins with a radio scanning through the stations. The drum machine (ever-present on the album) places the track firmly in its era. The production influence of Jimmy Jam and Terry Lewis' (then ruling the charts) is evident. This could almost be the beginning of a Janet Jackson track, although the cold, funky Jam/Lewis-like space is crowded with vocoder, guitar and synthesizer.

The lyric addresses the fast rat race that is life, with a few punches thrown at modern society along the way.

The human race is running over me
I punch a clock at nine and five
Just trying to make a livin'
A plastic face on satellite TV says 'Life is filled with give and take'
He's taking, and I'm giving

The chorus reveals the protagonist to have a system of survival – dancing. Essentially consisting of two chords, 'System Of Survival' is even more production-based than *Electric Universe*, and it appears that a lot more thought went into samples and synth patches than the songwriting itself. This style might've worked for late-1980s Coca Cola advertisements, but as an EW&F track, the result was largely underwhelming and forgettable.

The single reached 60 in the US – not exactly returning with a bang. The non-album B-side 'Writing On The Wall' featured a more established and catchy melody (and kalimba), and may have been a better choice for the A-side.

'Evil Roy' (Bailey, Willis, Giles)
'Evil Roy' became the album's second single but failed to hit the pop chart, reaching 38 on the Dance Club chart and 22 R&B. Philip Bailey and Allee Willis wrote it with Bailey's friend Attala Zane Giles – known for work with Miles Davis, Patti Austin and Larry Graham. A thumping one-chord vamp makes up the intro and verse, with a descending synth-bass riff and occasional guitar stabs lurking in the mix. Maurice takes the lead. A messy pre-chorus leads to an uninspired chorus hook.

Evil Roy
Who is fooling who?
Don't you know evil?
Evil Roy
Someone's watching you

The bridge adds a bit more melodic content, and an interesting instrumental section with jabbing keys leads to some great notes from Bailey and an excellent drum fill from Ricky Lawson.

'Thinking Of You' (White, Vaughn, Vaughn)
A chiming synthesizer opens this track. Lawson's drums are layered with an electronic rhythm to create a booming groove. The synth eventually descends into madness, climaxing with the drums before coming down to a rhythm that recalls Prince's 'Housequake' (released earlier that year). If the listener

is hoping for something different after the interesting beginning, they'll be disappointed. The verse melody is reasonable, but it soon becomes clear that the part Vaughn and Williams sing in the intro is actually the chorus, and the promise of any payoff quickly disappears.

Unfortunately, 'Thinking Of You' feels like it's one step behind the musical innovators of the time. It hit only 67 on the Hot 100, but reached three in the R&B.

'You And I' (Nevil, Mueller)
This was written by vocalist/guitarist Robbie Nevil – riding high from the success of his 1986 hit 'C'est La Vie' – and Mark Mueller, who later wrote the hit 'Crush' for Jennifer Paige. But it's little more than a sappy ballad. Bailey is in fine form, though, and it might work well for those seeking the group's more-romantic material.

'New Horizons (Interlude)' (Meyers)
The last track on side one is a two-minute instrumental interlude written by the track's co-producer Bill Meyers. Beginning with snippets of past EW&F hits, the rest sounds something like the soundtrack to a high-stakes scene from a 1980s action movie.

'Money Tight' (White, Willis, Sembello)
This lyric became something of a self-fulfilling prophecy on the subsequent tour. Lawson graces the track with his tight grooves combined with programmed drums. It turns out to be one of the album's more memorable tracks, despite dated synth horn and bass sounds. Maurice's verse leads to a pre-chorus hook that sticks in the mind more than the chorus that follows. A key change in the bridge adds drama, as does the following percussion-driven section. 'Money Tight' is no worse than the standard pop fare of the time, but it contains none of the classic EW&F hallmarks.

'Every Now And Then' (Lind, Walsh)
The killer session trio of Porcaro, East and Jackson Jr. return on a song co-written by Brock Walsh, who later worked on smash hits by artists like Christina Aguilera, Bette Midler and The Pointer Sisters. But being a slow-winding adult-contemporary track, 'Every Now And Then' seems destined to only appeal to fans of that genre, and slows the album's momentum to a crawl. Every step feels a little too predictable, and the song doesn't stack up against the group's similar late-1970s and early-1980s efforts.

'Touch The World' (Wells)
The title track finds Lawson on drums, East on bass, but this time George Duke on piano. Popular gospel vocal group The Hawkins Family provide thick vocals. But the production overshadows everything. The syrupy chorus

– though having powerful vocals – is too saccharine. It's great for those that are into the genre but not so great for everyone else.

'Here Today And Gone Tomorrow' (Bailey, Ballard, Sharron)

Another ballad doesn't help the album move along. Bailey's co-writers were Glenn Ballard – who later found huge success writing and producing Alanis Morrisette's *Jagged Little Pill* album – and Marti Sharron, who wrote for artists like The Pointer Sisters and Anita Baker. The track tries hard to be memorable but doesn't quite get there. Bailey's vocal is excellent throughout, but it's another big-ballad miss for EW&F.

'Victim Of The Modern Heart' (Prince)

The album closer brings a more up-tempo funky vibe to wrap up proceedings. It was written by Ian Prince, who'd made a name for himself by working with Al Jarreau and producing the soundtrack of the hit TV series *Baywatch*. Being more catchy than the majority of the album, 'Victim Of The Modern Heart' might've made a better single than the ones chosen, having a memorable chorus and some great horn lines.

Heritage (1990)

Personnel:
Maurice White: vocals, drums, kalimba
Verdine White: bass
Ralph Johnson: percussion
Philip Bailey: vocals
Sonny Emory: drums
Sheldon Reynolds: guitar, vocals
Andrew Woolfolk, Gary Bias: saxophone
Reggie Young: trombone
Ray Brown: trumpet
Producer: Maurice White
Executive producer: Bobby Colomby
Engineers: Dave Luke, Frankie Blue, Jesse Kanner, John Agnello, Les Pierce,
Mitch Gibson, Paul Klingberg, Rober Marcias
Studios: Ocean Way, Record One, Lion's Share, The Control Center, Fantasy
Studios, California; The Hit Factory, New York
Mixing: Jon Gass
Mastering: Eddie Schreyer
Release date: 17 February 1990
Chart positions: US: 70, US R&B/Hip Hop 19, UK: 18 (Blues & Soul)
Running time: 51:24

With the last album and tour not living up to the group or Columbia Records'
expectations, EW&F returned to the drawing board for 1990's *Heritage*.
Verdine was back onboard, too, having buried any ill will between him and
Maurice. Record company pressure resulted in a request that was becoming
commonplace for older 1990s acts. In *My Life With Earth, Wind & Fire*
Maurice later recalled: 'Columbia Records would push the group to include
hip hop elements in the album. They would suggest the group include
younger guest artists on our next album to hip things up. To show I had a
spirit of cooperation and that maybe I was hip too, I agreed: Big-ass mistake'.
Bailey was even more scathing in *Shining Star*:

We were clutching at straws when we released *Heritage* in February 1990 –
our final album on Columbia. It's filled with annoying drum machines and
in-board studio effects. And even special guests like MC Hammer (featured on
two tracks), a prepubescent rap group on Motown called The Boys, and an
aging Sly Stone couldn't rescue the dated and insincere studio sound of the
record. Hip hop was going full steam at the time, and there we were figuring
out if we could still play the game. It was our most-disappointing record. Ugh.

The album fared worse than *Touch The World* on the charts, peaking at 70.
The sound effects sent Maurice scrambling for more natural sources of music,

and – to get away from modern sounds – he later worked on jazz albums, including Ramsey Lewis' *Sky Island*, and *Urban Knights* with Lewis, Grover Washington Jr., Victor Bailey and Omar Hakim.

Unfortunately, this was overshadowed by a more devastating blow. Maurice remembered: 'I woke up one day in 1990, shaking. Around 1986, I started getting tiny hand tremors, but *this* morning was clearly different. It was a disturbing feeling'. He soon saw leading practitioners in alternative medicine, who all said he'd developed some kind of nerve disorder. By 1991, the tremors were worse, and Maurice lost trust in alternative medicine, doctors at L.A.'s USC hospital informing him he had Parkinson's disease in an extremely slow progression. He kept it secret for years, eventually making it public in 2000, telling *Rolling Stone*: 'I travelled with the band for five years with Parkinson's. I was treating it with medication then, and I still have it under control. It's not taking anything away from me'.

Bailey wasn't quite so optimistic: 'I noticed that he had begun taking strong medication. Then we experienced a very scary incident. In Amsterdam, we were crossing an avenue on which trolleys were running. I looked over and saw Maurice standing in the middle of the road as a speeding trolley headed directly toward him. I grabbed him and pulled him out of the way just in time'.

Tough times lay ahead for Maurice and the group. But first came the release of *Heritage*, which found them flailing for the second time since reuniting.

'Interlude: Soweto' (White)

The kalimba opens the album in an introduction that bears little indication of what's to come. Lasting barely 30 seconds, it's of little consequence.

'Takin' Chances' (Blue, Pierce)

Songwriters Frankie Blue and Leslie Pierce made a large contribution to *Heritage*, and both later worked with artists like Martika, Color Club and vocal ensemble Manhattan Transfer.

From the first notes, this sounds like the year it comes from, bearing little resemblance to the EW&F we'd come to know and love. In June 1990, Maurice told Kansas newspaper *Lawrence Journal-World* that the album was about 'musical heritage, the things we had drawn from. And we wanted to bring our fans' attention to things to appreciate; things to be proud of'. It's a great sentiment on paper, but the album didn't reflect this in the slightest. With new-jack swing being all the rage, the group's adoption of the sound felt forced. The young new-jack swing fans didn't want to hear a heritage act like EW&F – they had their own heroes to admire.

The verse melody is reasonably memorable, but Verdine's bass playing is not present at all. The chorus features Maurice responding – unconvincingly – to he and Bailey's vocals, in a modern, hip-hop-style inflection.

Unfortunately, the track comes across with more of a Pizza Hut advertisement vibe, than a good start to an album.

'Heritage' (White, Blue, Pierce)

The Boys – whom Bailey referred to as a 'pre-pubescent rap group on Motown', were exactly that – four brothers from California with a hit debut album produced by hitmakers L.A. Reid and Babyface. Their single 'Dial My Heart' peaked at 13 in the US, and was number one on the Hot R&B chart. Three years later, the bubble had burst, and their last effort under the name – 1992's *The Saga Continues* – scraped its way to 192. EW&F's bizarre duet with the group managed to hit five R&B, and was the album's highest-charting single.

Maurice and Philips' verse is unnecessarily – even annoyingly – followed by The Boys. The pre-chorus is surprisingly okay – Bailey and White trying their best to recapture the group's sound, a key change taking place before the chorus kicks in. The chorus, too, is well-written pop, countermelodies leading to an intense electronic showdown that ends with a high, steady note from Bailey. He takes over for the bridge, before a rap section from The Boys lets the air out of the track. Their turn at the chorus feels as if it's supposed to be cute, but it comes across as cringeworthy.

'Good Time' (White, Brookins, Stone)

'Good Time' is a slightly depressing listen, mainly due to the presence of fallen funk idol Sly Stone. Stone and his group The Family Stone became indisputably one of the greatest funk acts of all time following a string of legendary albums culminating in 1973's *Fresh*. But Sly fell on terribly hard times after that, suffering serious problems with addiction and finances. Here he sounds a shadow of his former self (despite the high scream he lets out during the introduction), effect filtering covering up his rough verses. The chorus is a non-event being minus a hook. 'Good Time' is probably best forgotten.

'Interlude: Body Wrap' (White)

A brief conversation between Sly and Maurice.

'Anything You Want' (Prince)

Ian Prince had worked with Quincy Jones on his *Back on the Block* album, and with Jermaine Jackson on *Don't Take it Personal*. Unlike his 'Victim Of The Modern Heart' on *Touch the World*, 'Anything You Want' is a slow-moving ballad. Smooth, muted horns lend some romance to the track, and an 808 drum machine supplies the groove. Maurice injects passion into the grinding verse rhythm, sounding more soulful than anywhere on *Touch The World*. The chorus appears after building to a tense crescendo from vocal trio Wanda Vaughn, Jeanette Hawes and Josie James. The chorus' vocal interplay and jazz movements are a breath of fresh air and the album's most musical section so far. It comes as no surprise that the album's first song that genuinely feels like EW&F is also its best.

'Interlude: Bird' (Bias)
Saxophonist Gary Bias takes a brief be-bop solo here, paying homage to all-time great Charlie 'Bird' Parker, and sounds excellent in the process.

'Wanna Be The Man ' (White, White, Reynolds, MC Hammer, Patterson)
Adding MC Hammer to the album was a no-brainer for Columbia Records – the young hip hop artist's new album *Please Hammer Don't Hurt 'Em'* had been released only the week prior. But what no one knew at the time was that his album was to have a lengthy stay at number one, and would become the genre's first to be certified as diamond (sales of 10,000,000). The album's third single, 'You Can't Touch This' – built around a direct sample of Rick James' 'Super Freak', became an international phenomenon, and MC Hammer became an emblem of the 1990s that's still referenced in popular culture today. But he was to crash hard after the fast rise, and by the end of the decade, found himself bankrupt.

The new-jack-swing groove returns while Hammer raps over the generic rhythm. 'Wanna Be The Man' really features nothing musically notable, Hammer's presence adding little to the vibe. Bloated and dated, the track really isn't worth the time it takes to listen to it, and was another corporate idea that just didn't work out.

MC Hammer took The EW&F Horns out on the tour for his hit album, and often discussed his love of the group in interviews.

The last single from the album, it reached 46 on the Hot R&B album chart.

'Interlude: Close To Home' (Mays)
This is a quick take on the melody from the piece by jazz keyboardist Lyle Mays, whose 1980s work with guitarist Pat Metheny was critically acclaimed. But this version now suffers from dated synth patches; the pan-pipe sound is a rough listen. It's a harmless break from the up-tempo tracks, despite not really fitting in.

'Daydreamin'' (White, Hill, Spears, Young)
The intro keyboard riff from 'Daydreamin'' was sampled by hip hop artist Nas on his track 'Pray', but was only available on the cassette release of his album *I Am* (surely another nod to EW&F).

The notes are played using a synthesizer string patch, and could have come straight from a Eurythmics track. Reynolds provides some hot licks once the groove has kicked in, and Maurice and Philip bring in the main hook:

Daydreamin' when I'm thinking of you
Missing all the things that we used to do
Dancing at the party on a Saturday night
It was cool

The groove itself is a slow burner, relaying the nostalgia of the lyric. The verse has a different melody and chords before it drifts to the chorus progression. The hooks are catchy and strong, the transition from the second chorus to the stripped-back intro being an example of attention-to-detail, and the album would've been better off with more of this style. Maurice and Philip sound more comfortable with this track's smooth R&B than the booming new-jack swing on the rest of the album. 'Daydreamin'' is another album highlight.

'King Of Groove' (Stewart)
This song by Ramsey Lewis alumnus Morris Stewart suffers from the same symptoms as much of the album, and is cut from the same cloth as Paula Abdul's 'Opposites Attract', with an almost cartoonish rhythm. The intense hi-hat programming may have been intended to sound like Prince's work on The Time's funk classic '777-9311', but is instead abrasive. But Maurice White does get one marvellous moment in – holding a single strong note for a good 15 seconds before descending into a run: a remarkable vocal display.

'I'm In Love' (Hill, Spears, Young)
'I'm In Love' is essentially a soft-ballad showcase for Philip Bailey, who sings great throughout, pouring passion into his vocals – but the song just isn't memorable. The keyboard sound gets old quickly, and the track fails to offer anything that would elicit a return.

'For The Love Of You' (White, MC Hammer, Patterson, Mills, Brookins)
MC Hammer returns for the album's lead single. Incredibly bland, none of the musical elements represent the EW&F sound, and the melody is monotonous. The track reached 19 R&B, but failed to hit the Hot 100, understandably. It's too far removed from what the group stood for to have made any impact, and a limp chorus does not help matters. MC Hammer turns in a half-baked performance during the bridge.

'Gotta Find Out' (Hill, Spears, Young)
By the time 'Gotta Find Out' rolls around, it's painfully clear that *Heritage* is thin on ideas. Again interchangeable with any of the album's up-tempo tracks, the song at least has some unusual chord changes in the chorus, though Maurice rapping 'Little Jack Horner/Sitting in the corner/Eating his curds and whey', just doesn't work.

'Motor' (White, Blue, Pierce)
The sound of a car starting up and speeding away opens 'Motor'. The melody and Maurice's performance are perfectly fine, and the chorus sounds sleek and smooth thanks to the vocal turns of Vaughn, James and Hawes. It's not overall one of the group's better tracks by any means.

'Interlude: Faith' (Young)
This instrumental interlude could easily be incidental music from the 1980s
TV show *Moonlighting*. With a running time of just over a minute, it comes
and goes before really developing into anything substantial.

'Welcome' (White, Young, Johnson)
'Welcome' features a great chord progression, though the production takes
it hostage. The more-natural drum feel helps, and the 32nd-note tom fills
pounding are an original touch. The problem is mainly with the track's
placement on the album, and the fatigue that has occurred by its arrival.

'Soweto (Reprise)' (White, Young, Johnson)
Bookending the album with the 'Soweto' interlude was a nice idea, but on an
album with minimal artist integrity, these gestures are a little pointless.

Millennium (1993)

Personnel:
Maurice White: vocals, drums, kalimba
Ralph Boyd Johnson, Paulinho da Costa: percussion
Philip Bailey: vocals
Sonny Emory: drums
Rex Selas, Darnell Spencer, Michael Thompson: bass
Don Wyatt, Jorge Strunz, Michael Thompson: guitar
Sheldon Reynolds: guitar, vocals
Andrew Woolfolk, Gary Bias: saxophone
Reggie Young: trombone
Ray Brown: trumpet
Arranger: Jerry Hey
Producer: Maurice White
Executive producer: Bobby Colomby
Engineers: Guy Fazio, Paul Klingberg, Mark Fergesen, Judy Kirschner
Studios: Andora, Capitol, Devonshire, Sonic Lab, California
Mixing: Mick Guzauski, Vachik Aghaniantz
Mastering: Steve Hall at Future Disc
Release date: 14 September 1993
Chart positions: US: 39, US R&B/Hip Hop 8, UK: -, Japan: 18
Running time: 1:03:32

The letdown that was *Heritage* severely compromised relations between
EW&F and Columbia Records to the point that Maurice actively looked to
leave. But after a successful with Warner Bros., the group were signed, with
Maurice promised creative control over the next album.

But Tragedy seemed to stalk the group in the early-1990s, and during the
making of *Millennium*, they were left in shock when sax master Don Myrick
(possibly best-known for his solo on Phil Collins smash hit 'One More Night')
was shot to death in his home on 30 July 1993. Upon knocking on Myrick's
door (in a case of mistaken identity), the police thought the cigarette lighter
in his hand was a gun, and murdered him in his doorway. His death and the
suspicion of racism surrounding it, left the group shaken. Myrick was buried
on 14 August 1993, the *Los Angeles Times* reporting the event as 'a jazzman's
funeral, but troubling questions about Myrick's life and death hung in the air
like the grating notes of an unresolved chord'. Larry Dunn said in the same
report that Myrick was 'shot down like a common criminal, it's ridiculous.
Most of the people here are still in shock'.

With *Millennium*, Maurice hoped to bring back the group's signature sound,
originally planning for the album to be their swansong. To accommodate
this return came some new songwriters, one being megastar Prince, whose
career Maurice had kept a close eye on since the very beginning when it was
proposed that he produce the virtuoso's debut album. The other name of note

is legendary songwriter Burt Bacharach – a towering figure responsible for more hits than can be mentioned here.

The album's artwork was an updated vision of the group's common themes of their golden age, with direction by Kim Champagne and illustrations by famed Japanese graphic designer Tananori Yokoo.

Upon release, *Millennium* was seen as a return to form, climbing higher than *Heritage*, to hit 39 on the *Billboard* 200, and receiving reviews ranging from moderate to glowing. Interestingly, the group's popularity in Japan now hit its highest point – *Millennium* reaching 18 there. The group capitalised on this with a large tour of the country.

But between these shows and two televised performances from the *American Music Awards* and *The Arsenio Hall Show*, the public was growing suspicious of Maurice's condition – his performances not being up to their usual standard. Eventually, the group decided that the best thing for their touring future and for Maurice's health, would be for EW&F to tour without him. Maurice retired from performing in 1994, the group forging ahead with Bailey as its focal point. Bailey recalled the shift in *Shining Star*:

> We aligned ourselves with Irving Azoff's Frontline Management. The central lineup became Verdine, Ralph and me as the original frontline triumvirate. We went on the radio to announce on Tom Joyner's nationally syndicated morning show, the news that we were back. We performed live in the studio, and Tom heartily endorsed the concept of EWF going out without Maurice. We negotiated a licensing agreement with Maurice so that we could legally use the name Earth, Wind & Fire. By 1996, EWF was back on the road without its original mentor and founder, but with a full musical ensemble: guitars, keyboards, drums, bass and the five-piece Earth, Wind & Fire Horns'.

After Maurice's retirement, Earth, Wind & Fire would never be the same, becoming an altogether different beast: a heritage act. But before that transformation was complete, fans had *Millennium* to sink their teeth into.

'Even If You Wonder' (White, Lind, Brown, Cohen)

As the opening track on an album that was supposedly a return to the group's roots, this intro sounds remarkably like the album that preceded it – that is, until the smooth, slightly mysterious chord changes of the verse arrives. The songwriting is a level up from the group's previous post-reunion efforts, and by the time the chorus rolls around the drum machine is overwhelmed by Verdine's bass and Maurice's sweet melody. The chorus keeps the hooks flowing, Bailey and Maurice blending just like in the group's heyday.

'Even If You Wonder' is still a different EW&F despite the promises. But it's a ton more reminiscent of the group's 1970s style than just about anything from the last couple of albums.

'Sunday Morning' (White, Willis, Reynolds)

Opening with a burst of horns and a jangling keyboard riff, the album's second single clawing its way to number 53 in the US, and 20 on R&B chart. The track immediately establishes its most memorable segment: the chorus. Replacing Verdine's synth bass may not have been the best choice soundwise, but the songwriting shines through. Countermelodies circle around the main title hook in a way the group hadn't done in years: perhaps thanks to old friend Allee Willis.

The same chords provide the bedrock for the verse – another memorable melody with Maurice taking the lead, embers of Reynolds' rock guitar burning slightly beneath the surface. The lyric is that of a simple love song – 'I'm forever anticipating your face on my pillow/You're the sunshine pourin' through my window'.

The EW&F Horns find a place in the instrumental bridge, before programming comes in with samples of the track's vocals scattered throughout. But even this section can't detract from the joyous feel, and the track rolls along unaffected, even including a false stop and some complex horn lines, just like the old days. Reynolds plays a bluesy solo before the chorus takes it out to the fade.

'Blood Brothers' (White, Lind, Brown, Walsh)

The 'Blood Brothers' intro comes even closer to the group's original sound – the EW&F Horns playing a funky riff over sparkling strings, while a nasty clavinet keeps the grooving rhythm turning over. The bass, too, sounds inspiring – full, round and tight. The verse is a little too tame to keep it up, sounding more like an up-tempo adult contemporary track. The lyric seems to be self-referential, Bailey taking the lead:

Voices from the past
Reunite at last
Back when we grew up on the streets
The world was at our feet
Do you recall the two of us
How we used to sing
When everything was new to us?

The track's chorus isn't bad, but the awkward pause before the title is sung takes the momentum out of the part.

Maurice opens with the lead on verse two until Philip returns for the chorus, and the intro returns before a soft, low, dynamic bridge leads back to the inevitable ending choruses and a fade on an instrumental of the section.

'Blood Brothers' doesn't live up to the promise of the opening tracks, but is still a fine effort from a group looking to turn back the clock.

'Kalimba Interlude' (White)
'Kalimba Interlude' is just that, and it's always a pleasure to hear Maurice playing the instrument.

'Spend The Night' (Thomas)
The album's lead single also became its highest-charting, reaching 42 Hot R&B and 36 Adult R&B. Written by up-and-coming gospel songwriter Dawn Thomas (who later worked with Anita Baker), 'Spend The Night' is extremely mushy, sounding something like a Christian-rock ballad, and stalling the album's forward momentum. The saccharine synth sounds and lyrics (much like the last album's issues) are, at this point, a bore, and the generic chorus feels like it could be interchanged with any number of other songs in the genre. The fiery instrumental parts in the bridge are the only real redeeming features here, but are not enough to make the song worth recommending to anyone but the most vigilant fan.

'Divine' (Bailey, Barken, Seeman)
'Divine' opens, sounding like the acid jazz movement from the UK. Groups and artists like Incognito, Jamiroquai and Ronny Jordan were pedalling a unique brand of funk/disco mixed with jazz and grounded in the acid-house club beats of the late-1980s. But once the verse begins, Bailey's inflections are total Prince, with occasional *Dangerous*-era Michael Jackson vibes. The pre-chorus keeps this going, before the chorus blows up with backing vocals and keys. Following the second chorus, Bailey really turns up for the bridge before a recurring bass lick ushers the chorus back in. It's the album's most memorable track, but it is a nice slice of the early-1990s.

'Two Hearts' (White, Bailey, Bacharach)
EW&F's collaboration with one of the most renowned songwriters is by no means the most sought-after of either act, and, unfortunately, feels phoned-in. Distracting electronic percussion is peppered with horns and synth strings. 'All my life, I've been told men don't show much emotion', Bailey croons over the half-time feel. Reynolds' guitar sometimes rears its head, along with some cheeky sax licks. The pre-chorus ups the ante with an ascending chord sequence and string-covered vocal lines, while the chorus itself is acceptable but doesn't really hit it out of the park. To end the bridge, Bailey reaches for the stars. His vocal performance is exceptional, adding some Michael Jackson style 'woo's before hitting some incredible notes during the fade-out.

Fans of Bacharach won't find much of worth here. 'Two Hearts' was the album's third and final single, and it only hit 88 on the R&B chart.

'Honor The Magic' (White, Ravel)
Written with the group's live musical director and keyboardist Freddie Ravel, 'Honor the Magic' is a quick diversion from the album sound so far, and is

best described as Latin jazz. Opening with percussion (which could have benefitted from a more-natural kick drum sound), Maurice soon comes in with a smooth melody, while a descending chord progression is played by electric piano. Bailey's backing vocal joins for the chorus, and eventually, he takes the lead with some passionate licks.

'Honor The Magic' is a fun track, and it's nice to hear the band explore territory they'd often experimented with in the 1970s.

'Love Is The Greatest Story' (White, Lawrence, Freenberg)
Co-writers David Lawrence and Faye Greenburg later worked on Disney's *High School Musical* films, and it shows here on one of the album's most dated tracks. A poor brass patch plays the main melody before Maurice takes over for the verse. This just doesn't really work out, and is an unnecessary throwback to the last album *Heritage*.

'The 'L' Word' (White, Willis, Lind, Brown)
With a sci-fi synth introduction that does its best to sound like Larry Dunn has returned, 'The 'L' Word' loses its appeal incredibly fast, and is one of the album's low points. This might've worked better on a *Teenage Mutant Ninja Turtles* soundtrack than this album, and with the group set on using the entire CD length, the listener may start growing tired 'round-about now'.

'Just Another Lonely Night' (Stokes, Stokes)
Producer/songwriter Michael Stokes – known for his work with Smokey Robinson and Maurice's old pal Booker T. Jones – wrote this song with his wife Linda, known for her work with former Motown recording artists Magic Lady. 'Just Another Lonely Night' shows the album's other ballad writers how it's done, giving Bailey an excellent vehicle while nodding to the funk and soul grooves that were the backbone of EW&F's greatest tracks.

The song would sound even better with less-intense production, but for the era, it works well. Over a funky bass line, Bailey intones a simple lyric of lost love, recalling his lover 'searching for a better life in L.A.'. The chorus features a strong vocal hook, nice guitar work from Reynolds, a lot of sampled brass sounds, and tends to stay with the listener. The track saves the album after some big slip-ups.

'Super Hero' (Nelson)
This is a dream collaboration and a meeting of funk icons. There are few names in music bigger than Prince and Earth, Wind & Fire. But that the partnership happened in this particular era, should temper expectations. This is neither act's best-remembered era – a reminder coming from the booming drum loop and circus-like opening riff, though the bass line gives some grounding. Funky guitar and horns weave in and out of the arrangement, and Prince is prominent in the mix – also credited with keys and programming.

The verse melody makes it clear that the track began life as a Prince demo, and Maurice doesn't sound too comfortable with the minimal note movement, giving off the opposite vibe to Prince's incredible nonchalance.

An instrumental bridge contains some excellent layered horn lines that make the track feel like it's on the verge of a breakdown before Prince absolutely rips it up on guitar. Maurice sounds more comfortable in the next verse, bringing more of himself to the table. A quasi-operatic style section begins towards the end (bringing to mind Prince's own mini-epic of the time: '3 Chains O' Gold'), and the song fades on the chorus.

Prince later re-recorded the track with his group The New Power Generation and vocal group, The Steeles, for the soundtrack to the Damon Wayans movie *Blankman*.

'Wouldn't Change A Thing About You' (Bailey, Blue)
The lyrics of 'Wouldn't Change A Thing About You' are sappy and slightly corny ('If I were king and I ruled the world/I'd make it safe for the boys and girls'), but the melody is worthwhile. The chorus feels like an extended pre-chorus – dragging on but never quite going anywhere. Its uptempo, easy-going pop style doesn't impact the listener in a negative way, however, it's nearly instantly forgettable, and its inclusion isn't much appreciated here, unfortunately.

'Love Across The Wire' (White, Bailey, Bell)
This verse is forgettable, but the key change in the chorus is a nifty trick. But synth brass badly dates the track, coming across as bloated and unnecessary. This kind of track worked best for EW&F, sparingly – maybe once or twice on an album – and their constant effort to recapture the magic of 'Reasons' or 'After The Love Has Gone' on every second track, grows stale.

'Chicago (Chi-Town) Blues' (White, Lind, Brown, Walsh)
The lyric reminisces about growing up, and brings up some nostalgia:

> Booker T.'s at the front door
> Saying it's time to go
> Coltrane's at the Mother Blues tonight

But the good intentions don't really translate to anything musically noteworthy, and, again, this kind of thing would sound much better without the drum reverb and synthesizers – a genuine EW&F-style blues would be a treat. The horn section *does* sound great, and the 'ba di a' throwback of the chorus is a nice turn, but none of it is enough to make the track required listening.

'Kalimba Blues' (White)
Maurice plucks away at the kalimba, finally closing the lengthy album.

In The Name of Love (1997)

Personnel:
Maurice White: vocals, drums, kalimba, percussion
Ralph Johnson: drums, percussion, vocals
Philip Bailey: vocals, congas, percussion
Verdine White: bass, percussion, vocals
Carl Carwell: vocals
Sonny Emory: drums
Sheldon Reynolds: guitar, vocals
Additional Musicians:
Morris Pleasure, Mike McKnight, Andrew Klippel, Damian Johnson, Marcel East, Paul Minor: keyboards
David Romero, David B. Butterworth: percussion
Scott Mayo: saxophone
Bill Reichenbach, Reggie Young: trombone
Gary Grant, Jerry Hey: trumpet
Producer: Maurice White
Mixing: Don Murrey
Studios: Andrew Scheps Studio, Sony, Sunset Sound, California
Mastering: Wally Traugott at Tower Mastering
Release date: 22 July 1997
Chart positions: US: 50 (R&B), UK: 19 (R&B)
Running time: 48:52

Despite *Millennium* going over well with fans, the lack of sales drove Warner Bros. to drop the band, after only one album. *In The Name of Love* was released through the smaller independent label Pyramid Records.

 Though the group had essentially been downsized, they intended a return to their roots, as had been the plan with *Millennium*. The live show had also changed greatly, with guitarist Sheldon Reynolds taking most of Maurice' vocals. Saxophonist Andrew Woolfolk had departed in early-1996. New musicians added to the lineup included keyboard players Morris Pleasure and Mike McKnight, percussionists David Butterworth and David Romero, and backing vocalist Carl Carwell. Carwell was good friends with Philip Bailey since they grew up together in Denver, and also knew Larry Dunn in his youth. Maurice was still perfectly capable of working in the studio (and occasionally popped up for special live performances), continuing to sing, play and produce the band.

 Unfortunately, the press for this album was almost non-existent, the group seeming to barely remember the release themselves – it is seldom mentioned in interviews and receives zero acknowledgment in either Maurice or Phillip's autobiographies. Fans were more fond of *In The Name of Love* than *Millennium,* but the former was far from a return to form. It was first released in Japan under the title *Avatar* (the cover an ankh symbol against a purple and blue background) during the last half of 1996 to capitalise on the group's recent boost in popularity there. *Avatar* reached 25 in Japan: a respectable position for a low-key release. With a different track listing for the rest of the world, *In The Name of Love* hit record stores on 22 July 1997, hitting 50 R&B in the US, and 19 R&B in the UK. Although the album is unavailable to stream, CDs are easily found. The readily-available 2006 reissue includes the *Avatar*-only track 'Change Your Mind', which hit 26 on the Adult R&B chart.

'Rock It' (Bailey, White, Reynolds, Emory, Pleasure)
'Rock It' opens with a descending three-note bass riff over a 1990s hip hop groove. The spoken words 'EWF comin' at ya' 96 style' sound forced and unnatural for the group, and are particularly cringeworthy. The verses are a letdown, Reynolds intoning in a drawl. The title may suggest more rock moments from *Faces* and surrounding albums, but instead, the listener is met with a half-baked track more suited for live than the studio. There *is* some great jazz sax from Scott Mayo, but not a lot else to recommend here.

'In The Name Of Love' (White, Reynolds, Pleasure, Andrews)
The title track begins suspiciously for an album being promoted as a return to the group's original sound – another modern drum loop, with a record scratch on the first beat of every bar (much like House of Pain's hit 'Jump Around' a few years prior). The EW&F horns sound great, but an annoying phaser effect upsets the mix a little too much. Maurice takes the lead, at one point quoting the melody from 'Jupiter', as if to highlight the album's throwback intention. But, again, the music doesn't match up, and despite the best intentions, nothing sticks. The chorus' weak hook falls flat. Bailey sounds great in the bridge and in the backing vocal, but the track has nothing for the audience to sink their teeth into.

'Revolution' (White, Bailey, Emory, Pleasure)
The introduction of 'Revolution' sounds more promising than the last two tracks, but it ends up as just another one-chord vamp over a similar groove. It was the album's lead single, landing at 89 on the Hot R&B chart.
Reynolds takes the lead vocal, his crooning as smooth as you can get, but there is minimal thought put into the songwriting. The verse groove remains the same throughout the chorus, though there is a chord change every second bar. The chorus hook is again forgettable, and a rap section in the bridge tries its best to save the song, but comes up well short. 'Revolution' feels pointless and undercooked.

'When Love Goes Wrong' (Bailey, Glass, Klippel)
A slow-burning R&B track, this wouldn't sound out of place on a Boyz II Men album. As the album's second single, it fared slightly better than 'Revolution', coming in at 33 Adult R&B.

A light section of harp opens the track before Bailey lets the chorus out of the bag right away. The group performs the verse well, and the melody is well-written, but this may not be what fans are looking for from EW&F. Again, the instrumentation doesn't really change from verse to chorus, bar some rising keyboard chords. That being said, Bailey is in his element here: sounding brilliant in a way only *he* can.

'Fill You Up' (Johnson, Minor, Tresvant, Guillaume, Hawkins Jr.)
Written by an army of outside writers, including television star Kevin Guillaume (son of actor Robert Guillaume), 'Fill You Up' is home to some great horn lines, but just never quite sticks. The slow-grind stomp is fine, but there's not a lot of the EW&F sound going on here, buried in an album that bears that problem overall. Once again, there is little to musically distinguish the verse from the chorus, bar the vocals.

'Right Time' (White, Reynolds, Minor, Andrews)
'Right Time' is another adult-contemporary ballad. Bailey's breathy vocal carries the track, bringing the wedding-reception vibes to an all-time high. The chorus features some nice backing vocals and a reasonable hook, while the bridge is the climax before endless choruses take the track out. It's ultimately another forgettable track to throw on the pile since the group's reunion.

"Round And 'Round' (Mayo, Wheaton)
This was written by saxophonist Scott Mayo and songwriter Will Wheaton, who'd worked with Diana Ross, Kenny Loggins and Quincy Jones. A synthetic flute sound begins the track, dating it in the worst way possible straight out of the gate. But a nice scat vocal/guitar line rescues it, though the verse – sung by Reynolds – brings the energy down and it never quite rises during the chorus, remaining stuck in its half-time groove. Essentially a showcase for Reynolds – who does give a great performance – "Round and 'Round' doesn't leave much of an impression.

'Keep It Real' (White, Reynolds, Pleasure, Andrews, Minor)
By this point, the album's songwriting formula is getting pretty old – 'Keep It Real' being interchangeable with any of the album's more-funky mid-to-up-tempo tracks. It has great playing and singing, but the songwriting just isn't there – the only silver lining being the bridge with Bailey singing over mildly-interesting chord changes. 'Keep It Real' is best left alone.

'Cruising' (Bailey, Emory, Pleasure, Seeman)
A brooding and mysterious ballad, Bailey takes the driver's seat on 'Cruising'. It's about as atmospheric as EW&F get – chords rising back and forth under Bailey's breathy vocals. A subdued jazz-like chorus keeps the mood going –

the band working the quiet-storm genre in their favour. Bailey's descending melody grabs the ear with its flawless execution. A soft drum groove begins in the second verse: brushes washing over the snare like raindrops. By stepping a little out of the box, while staying true to their jazz roots, 'Cruising' achieves what the rest of the album couldn't – the group sound like themselves.

'Love Is Life' (White, Flemons, Whitehead)
This is a retread of the song originally heard on the group's eponymous debut album. This updated version is perfectly serviceable if a tad unnecessary. The spirit and energy of the original are stripped away by the production and session players, losing the character that made the song special in the first place.

'Avatar' (Johnson, East)
The final track, 'Avatar' is nothing more than relaxing new age sounds and rhythms that would sound appropriate in a tarot-card-reading shop. You can almost smell the incense wafting in the air as a smooth sax solo drifts above the track. Though it's an interesting way to end the album, maybe it would've worked better as an interlude between tracks as it had on the Japanese *Avatar* release, or perhaps just left on the cutting room floor.

The Promise (2003)

Personnel:
Maurice White: vocals, drums, kalimba, percussion
Ralph Johnson: drums, percussion, vocals
Philip Bailey: vocals, congas, percussion
Verdine White: bass, percussion, vocals
Carl Carwell: vocals
John Paris: drums
Paulinho da Costa: percussion
Additional Musicians:
Wanda Vaughn, Wayne Vaughn: backing vocals
John Johnson, Bobby Gonzalez, Darrell Crooks, Gregory Moore, Carlos Rios, Eric Walls: guitar
Robert Brookins, Myron McKinley, Alan Hewitt, Wayne McKinley: keyboards
David Romero, Daryl Jackson, David B. Butterworth: percussion
Gerald Albright, Gary Bias: saxophone
George Bohanon, Andrew Martin, Reggie C. Young: trombone
Oscar Brashear, Ray Brown, Gary Grant, Jerry Hey: trumpet
Producers: Maurice White, Preston Glass
Engineer: Wallace Mercer
Studio: Magnet Vision, California
Mixing: Tim Kelly, Dexter Simmons
Mastering: Steve Hall at Magnet Vision
Release date: 20 May 2003
Chart positions: US: 89, 19 (R&B), UK: -
Running time: 56:42

The turn of the millennium saw Earth, Wind & Fire recognised by the Rock and Roll Hall of Fame, inducted by hip hop superstar Lil' Kim on 6 March 2000. The event saw the classic lineup return to the stage for one last time, to recapture the magic.

Unfortunately, it was to be a one-off moment, as the former members headed their own ways after the show. Maurice recalled in his autobiography:

The crowd got to their feet and applauded for what seemed to me too long. I was sincerely moved by their appreciation. I was even more moved by the eight applauding gentlemen standing behind me – Verdine White, Larry Dunn, Philip Bailey, Al McKay, Ralph Johnson, Andrew Woolfolk, Johnny Graham and Fred White. These were the men who took the journey with me, creating a new and powerful cross-cultural sound in pop music. On this weekend, we were all reminded by colleagues and fans that Earth, Wind & Fire had come to represent something more. We had indeed gained a new transcendent success.

In the weeks leading up to the event, Maurice divulged his disease to the media – a move he came to regret because that press coverage somewhat overshadowed the induction itself. Nonetheless, entering the Rock and Roll Hall of Fame was a good thing for the group.

In the following years, the live lineup evolved again, most notably with Sheldon Reynolds- arguably the most important of the recent members – leaving the fold in 2002 to concentrate on other projects. Bailey commented positively on the state of the touring act, to *Tokyo Weekender Magazine:* 'Oh, they are great. You know, we play an hour before a show because it's fun. Even at soundchecks, we are playing. I don't know any mailman who delivers mail on a day off just because it is fun'.

In 2002, Maurice called the group back to the studio for their first recording in six years. *The Promise* was recorded at his new facility Magnet Vision, and released on his label Kalimba Records. With old friends The Emotions on board for the lead single 'All The Way', the group marketed the album as another return to their original sensibilities. Critics and fans received it warmly – *The Guardian's* review (and many others) enthusiastic but tempered:

The Promise is Earth, Wind & Fire's best record for years. 17 tracks of immaculately-smooth, meticulously-detailed mid-tempo pop-soul, and thoroughly intoxicating in its lushness. Still led by Maurice White – who wrote and produced much of *The Promise* (but no longer tours since the onset of Parkinson's disease) – the band are unlikely to experience a renaissance to match their heyday.

The album tour was a success, and Maurice appeared at certain promotional stops along the way – for example, performing the new single 'All The Way' with the full band on CBS' *The Early Show.* Philip Bailey spoke about the new album when interviewed on the show: 'We had to find the songs, and then you find them and start to subtract from that. After a while, the months started to add up, but we finally got it done'.

'All The Way' (White, Vaughn, Vaughn, Vaughn)

The Promise opens with lead single 'All The Way', featuring The Emotions on backing vocals. It hit 77 R&B and 25 Adult Contemporary. It also happens to find the band sounding revitalised and unhampered by production using modern sounds. The kalimba showers the intro with notes, and when the main stomping groove appears, the music fluctuates mainly between two chords. The EW&F Horns sound tighter than ever, and hearing The Emotions sweet sounds on the opening chorus, is an album-defining moment. Maurice doesn't sound quite as sprightly as he did in his youth, but his tone is like a fine, matured wine. It's a greatly promising album opening.

'Betcha' (White, Glass)

Electric piano opens 'Betcha', co-writer Preston Glass perhaps doing his best to conjure a bit of Larry Dunn's magic. Bubbling, intergalactic sounds open the door for a marvellous Philip Bailey performance, washing cymbals and strings rising and falling beneath him. It all happens over an up-tempo groove, perhaps influenced by dominant R&B vocal acts of the time, such as Destiny's Child.

Betcha' come looking for me
'Cause girl, you know I really love you
Betcha' come looking for me
'Cause I know just how to satisfy you'

The second verse finds the rhythm bringing the chord changes to life, and Bailey sounds timeless in the bridge. 'Betcha" sounds like the group have woken up and remembered who they are, and they are all the better for it.

'Wiggle' (Glass)

'Wiggle' is a brief interlude of the variety the group are so fond of. There's a bouncing bass riff, as kalimba rings out into the night. The run-time of only 39 seconds may leave the listener wanting more, and it would've been interesting to hear where it might've gone were it more developed.

'Why?' (White, Curtis)

The album's fourth single was a co-write between Maurice, and Gregory Curtis, who later worked with Destiny's Child, Christina Aguilera and Raphael Saadiq, among others. Here he brings a smouldering but ultimately-soaring ballad to the table. A slow rhythm keeps the track moving, while Maurice takes the lead: 'Do you feel what I feel when you look at me?'. Bailey joins for the chorus, the backing vocals punctuating the melody with cries of 'Why?'. Maurice and Bailey have some nice vocal interaction during the bridge – an arrangement element sadly lacking since their golden years.

'Why?' may be simple in form compared to some similar earlier tracks, but it's no less potent. The single hit 19 on the Smooth Jazz chart in the US.

'Wonderland' (Simms, Rodriguez)

A heavy gospel influence is evident in 'Wonderland', thanks to the soulful organ. The acoustic guitar brings a modern sound, but the chords still feel like EW&F, and Bailey sounds great in his introductory *ad libs*. But the real highlight here is the work of vocalist Angie Stone, found here not long after the release of her classic *Mahogany Soul* album. Her vocals in the second verse – and layered with Maurice and Philip in the chorus – are top-tier. The singing that ends the bridge is truly inspiring, as are the chorus's vocal inflections. A breezy horn line plays during the fade, ending 'Wonderland' with the listener feeling satisfied.

'Where Do We Go From Here?' (Meyers, Vannelli)
Bill Meyers and Gino's brother Ross Vanelli return as co-writers on 'Where Do We Go From Here', and turn in a well-written track. Unfortunately, the chosen drum sounds slightly hamper the mood, and instrumentation more along the lines of the opening track would've suited it better. That being said, the gorgeous chord changes give Bailey a good platform to work with, and the string arrangement adds a sweeping soundscape to the back of the mix. The chorus melody is not highly memorable, and DJ-scratching and vocal effects after the mid-section, date the track. But it's still much better than the worst tracks of the *Heritage* era.

'Freedom' (White)
Another interlude, with percussion, kalimba, and some light vocals from Maurice. 'Freedom' doesn't add to the album, nor does it subtract, though it's not as memorable as 'Wiggle'.

'Hold Me' (Kelley, Robinson)
Following 'Where Do We Go From Here?', this track adds to the growing feel of a mid-album slump. The generic lyric feels insincere, and the limp loop that makes up the groove would've been better served by actual players (which the group did have at the time). Puzzlingly chosen as the album's second single, it reached 28 Adult R&B chart, but was not an ideal choice.

'Never' (White, Curtis)
Gregory Curtis again comes through with the goods – the album's third single 'Never' blowing away the cobwebs from the past few tracks, resuscitating the album in the process. Bailey takes the lead over the triumphant chord progression, and the Latin-sounding chords add a lot to the vocal melody. The chorus is catchy and a relief at this point in the album. Again, it would've been nice to hear a real drum kit and some fills instead of a drum loop, but this was 2003. Not as memorable as the lead single 'All The Way', 'Never' was still a much better choice than the momentum-stalling 'Hold Me', and hit 17 on the *Billboard* Smooth Jazz chart.

'Prelude' (White, Johnson, Crossley)
This is the third interlude in a short space of time. It's essentially a 40-second loop, with one bass note and one synth note added for good measure, but doesn't really add anything to the album.

'All About Love' (Vaughn, Vaughn, Hutchinson)
This slow burner could've been better if it was a bit faster, but the writing of the Vaughns and Sheila Hutchinson is always welcome – despite a rather-forgettable verse counteracted by some odd jazz-vocal intervals in the chorus. 'All About Love' sees the albums making the mistake of maintaining a slow

109

tempo when the listener needs a jolt in the arm, and you can't help but wonder where the floor-on-the-floor of a track like 'In The Stone' has gone. The Emotions still sound great, though.

'Suppose You Like Me' (Bailey, Thompson, Palladino, Poyser, Storch)
These writing credits might've intrigued fans before they even heard a bar of the music. Drummer Ahmir Thompson – more commonly known as Questlove (and most likely the most popular drummer of the last two decades) – keyboardists James Poyser and Scott Storch, and bassist Pino Palladino (whose credits are too numerous to list here, though has recently been seen with The Who and Nine Inch Nails) – were all members of The Soulquarians. A backing group for stars like Erykah Badu and D'Angelo, The Soulquarians are credited with helping form the sound known as neo-soul. Questlove and Poyser found further fame in the backing group for *The Tonight Show Starring Jimmy Fallon*. Here they co-write with Philip Bailey and play their respective instruments. That the live-band tracks are consistently more-listenable than the loop-driven songs, is hard to deny at this point.
    Bailey takes the lead, going back and forth with the backing vocals while the band lays down a groove strong enough to build a city on. The mysterious chord changes give the verse a vaguely-ethereal vibe, before the group accents bring about a short pre-chorus.
    Unfortunately, 'Suppose You Like Me' doesn't live up to the giant names that play on it.

'The Promise' (White, Johnson, Crossley)
Another drum loop with kalimba forms the title track, fading in and out, and only 27 seconds in length. The kalimba riff is surprisingly catchy, and may stick with the listener for a while.

'She Waits' (Harris, Simms)
'She Waits' opens with vocal equalisation within the frequency range of a telephone. Chiming chords and percussion keep the mood low, but soon the rhythm and stabbing horn section arrive to bring the track to life. The simple chorus hook is effective, and a great bass line underpins the percussion. The dynamic again comes down for the verse, staying low for the ensuing chorus. But the real surprise of 'She Waits' comes in the bridge when it dives headlong into hard rock – the rock guitar is a welcome sound and an important element of the original group that's been largely ignored on the album until this point. 'She Waits' might go down better had they trimmed some of the less impressive tracks and we arrived at it sooner, but its epic feel is undeniable.

'The Promise (Continued)' (White, Johnson)
This a continuation of the prior interlude, reinforcing the little melody.

'Let Me Love You' (Curtis)

The bustling 2003 feel of 'Let Me Love You' suffers from the same issue that much of the album does – the group sounding nowhere near as inspired when recording over a loop as opposed to a real rhythm section. The songwriting is fine, but it doesn't really stand out from the pack. Here Maurice arrives at his most impressive moment of vocal power on the album – which is worth the price of admission alone – but the track does little to inspire repeat listens.

'Dirty' (White)

'Dirty' begins with a dive-bombing guitar note, and one of Verdine's high vibrato bass notes, which were heard less often by this point. A drum loop that may give listeners *Heritage* or *Touch The World* flashbacks, begins to play, and it soon becomes clear that 'Dirty' is nothing more than a track to jam over. Maurice eventually tells a story about a guy called Dirty. The delay punctuating certain words is unintentionally hilarious. Eventually, some jazz changes are brought in to spice things up, and The EW&F horns sound excellent throughout. But nothing can shake the feeling that 'Dirty' sounds like incidental music made for television.

Illumination (2005)

Personnel:
Maurice White: vocals, drums, kalimba, percussion
Ralph Johnson: drums, percussion, vocals
Philip Bailey: vocals, congas, percussion
Verdine White: bass, percussion, vocals
Kim Johnson: vocals
John Paris: drums
Greg Moore, Vadim Zilberstein : guitar
David B. Butterworth: percussion, vocals
Myron McKinley: keyboards
Gary Bias: saxophone
Additional Musicians:
Gary Grant, Jerry Hey, Matt Cappy, Nolan Shaheed: trumpet
Reggie C. Young: trombone
Shorty B.: guitar
Kelvin Wooten, Preston Crump: bass
Prescott Ellison: drums
Bobby Ross Avila, Myron McKinley, Dave Robbins, Junius Bervine: keyboards
Producers: Maurice White, Jimmy Jam, Terry Lewis, Raphael Saadiq, Darren
Henson, Keith Pelzer, Brian McKnight and Organized Noize, Doc Holiday, Vikter
Duplaix, Walter Afanasieff
Executive producer: Philip Bailey
Engineers: Cameron Marcarelli, Ian Cross, James Tanksley, Tim Wentzlaff, Cha
Cha Jones, Jimmy Randolph, Sean Davis
Mixing: Neal H. Pogue, Matt Martin, Danny Romero, Manny Marroquin, Serban
Ghenea
Studios: Magnet Vision, Flyte Tyme West at The Village Recorders, Blakeslee
Recording Co., Larrabee North, Glenwood Place, KeffenDeez Place, Fire House
Studios, Los Angeles; The Dungeon, East Recording, Atlanta; Luminous Sound,
Texas
Mastering: Brian Gardiner at Bernie Grundman Mastering
Release date: 20 May 2005
Chart positions: US: 32, 8 (R&B), UK: -
Running time: 59:57

After the vintage patches of *The Promise, Illumination* comes with a looming
shadow that only retroactive listeners could appreciate. It was to be the
group's last work with Maurice, who retired from recording due to his
declining health. After years of piloting the band through good and bad times,
the band leader moved further into the shadows, leaving the trio of Philip
Bailey, Verdine White and Ralph Johnson to continue the band's mission.

But first came *Illumination* – an updated attempt at pairing the group with
modern musicians. It was released on UK label Sanctuary Records – at the

time, one of the largest independent labels in the world. Sanctuary effectively promoted the album, and helped the group make chart reappearances in the US and some European countries. The list of special guests included Big Boi (Outkast), Kelly Rowland (Destiny's Child), will.i.am (Black Eyed Peas), British duo Floetry, producer/musician Raphael Saadiq and vocalist Brian McKnight. Ralph Johnson spoke of the guests in an NPR radio interview: 'The writers and producers who came on board to help us do this, were fans of the band. They all have stories about seeing our shows back in the day, and how it affected them, and I think it really had a great effect on the end result'.

The idea paid off, with *Illumination* reaching 32 on the Billboard 200 and 8 on the R&B album chart. The reviews at the time were reasonably positive overall, and the album was well-received by fans, even if the all-encompassing classic run of albums by the original lineup overshadow it. But *Illumination* is a product of its time, and artists such as will.i.am interact with EW&F in a way that's not necessarily compatible with their advanced harmony.

'Lovely People' (will.i.am, Harris)
Reversed kalimba opens *Illumination*, sounding like a strange play on a sound we're so used to hearing from EW&F. The track that fires up shortly after is a bright start to the album. A simple groove underpins this song written by will.i.am and Black Eyed Peas producer Keith Harris, accented by some tight, punchy horn lines. The music remains static for much of the track; the same chord progression rolling on. Unfortunately, the lyric suffers from the same simplicity as much of the Black Eyed Peas catalogue. The track's low point comes in the form of will.i.am's rapped bridge and his brief attempt at scatting – almost laughable when considering the company he's in. 'Lovely People' starts the album off in a good mood but feels bland at the same time.

'Pure Gold' (Harris, Lewis, Avila, Avila, Tolbert)
'Pure Gold' begins with classic soul-style chord stabs, with some smooth vocals from Maurice, who sounds in fine form throughout. Jimmy Jam and Terry Lewis bring an excellent groove to the table, and the track feels more natural than 'Lovely People' did. The borderline neo-soul feel fits the more-mature EW&F well: a testament to Jam and Lewis' production savvy. Bailey takes the verse, and is in fine form as usual, slowly building up to the chorus, which explodes in a burst of old-school EW&F percussion and backing vocals. Hearing Maurice belt out the vocal licks feels special, knowing in hindsight that this was his last album with the group. The lyric feels more weighty and more age-appropriate than will.i.am's effort, Maurice pleading with the listener:

Won't you wake up, wake up
Walk in the light
Won't you wake up, wake up
Bring substance in your life

'Pure Gold' might've made for a better opening track than 'Lovely People'. This is a modern track, but unmistakably EW&F, right down to Bailey's incredible outro vocals.

Released as the album's third single, 'Pure Gold' hit 23 Adult Contemporary and 76 Hot R&B.

'A Talking Voice Interlude' (Bailey)
The quirky piece consisting of *a cappella* vocals lasts for 20 seconds, with Bailey showing what he can do in a manner reminiscent of the work of Bobby McFerrin and Al Jarreau.

'Love's Dance' (Harris, Lewis, Tolbert)
'Love's Dance' keeps up the precedent set by 'Pure Gold'. Funky guitar and cowbell scatter across the groove, the EW&F Horns flying high with their Jerry Hey-arranged parts. Bailey goes low for the verse, but is back in familiar high territory for the pre-chorus, calling and responding to himself. The chorus grows and swells, multi-layered Bailey vocals lifting the song up. The only element that hasn't aged well is Bailey's looped 'Gonna get get get, get on down' line after the chorus. This is counteracted by Maurice's soaring melody during the bridge, the *All 'N All*-era style seeping through. The reverence that Jam and Lewis have for the group is evident in the production and the songwriting. Again, they capture the album's mission statement, and hearing a whole album with Jam and Lewis would've made for excellent listening.

'Show Me The Way' (Saadiq, Jackson)
The album's second single, 'Show Me The Way' hit 16 on the Adult R&B chart. It was produced by prolific R&B artist Raphael Saadiq, who originally rose to fame as a member of Tony! Toni! Toné!, later producing hits for D'Angelo and Erykah Badu in addition to Saadiq's acclaimed solo work. This track keeps the neo-soul feel, with Saadiq's unique touch and ambitions shining through (the drums, in particular, bringing the vibes of his past work).

'Show Me The Way' is EW&F's longest track in a while, clocking in at nearly eight minutes. Maurice is caught on voicemail briefly before the groove kicks in, and then he picks up the verse with a catchy melody as the chords swim around beneath him. In what must be a career highlight, Saadiq takes over for the second half, his tone giving the track a slight lift. The chorus features a sweet, memorable melody, with Bailey at the top of the backing vocals creating a dreamy atmosphere.

The lyric deals with love in all its facets, Saadiq even fitting a spoken-word section in to really drill this home. The arrangement eventually breaks down to a bass-and-drums groove, with quiet guitar chords for good measure. Saadiq pivots to a slightly different melody here, multiple vocals low in the mix, drawing the listener in before the full rhythm comes back, this time with Bailey at the upper reaches of his range. By this point, the listener is convinced that – like Jam and Lewis – Saadiq understands what makes EW&F tick, and is fully capable of applying that to the present time.

'This Is How I Feel' (Brown, Patton, Etheridge, Murray, Wade)
Hit-making production trio Organized Noize (consisting of Sleepy Brown, Rico Wade and Ray Murray) take the wheel for 'This Is How I Feel'. Recent years had seen the team come up with massive hits such as 'Waterfalls' for TLC and 'So Fresh, So Clean' for Outkast, along with numerous others. The track opens with Outkast member Big Boi rapping over a relaxed beat, before Bailey comes in with the chorus line, soon joined by former Destiny's Child member Kelly Rowland, whose powerful vocal doesn't fail to impress. But 'This Is How I Feel' gets caught up in its own production, and it heads nowhere.

'Work it Out' (Bailey, Saadiq, Jackson, Wooten)
Saadiq's second track veers further into the neo-soul sub-genre, perhaps a little too much, and could be mistaken for his solo work. It's not a bad song by any means – in fact, the opposite is true of the track's snaking groove and twinkling piano quarter-notes. There are also great vocals throughout. Again, the biggest issue is the lack of signature EW&F elements, but it is thoroughly enjoyable, and recommended to fans of Saadiq's work.

'Pass You By' (Saadiq, Jackson)
This is Saadiq's third effort for the album – co-written with songwriter/producer Taura Stinson (notable for her work with Destiny's Child and Kelis). It opens starkly with bare guitar chords, soon transforming into a filled-out rhythm. The jaunty, descending chord pattern is accompanied by the restrained vocal line, 'Don't let love pass you by, pass you by'. Bailey's sweet vocal expertly navigates around the verse – the sound of longing in his voice is palatable. When the chorus returns, it's with added percussion helping to build the thumping rhythm. The multi-layered vocals of the outro are genuinely impressive, and the group sound as impressive as they ever did after 1988. Saadiq again succeeds in blending the old with the new.

'The One' (Bennett, Brown, Christian, Murray, Wade)
The production team of Organized Noize is back for 'The One'. A looped orchestra sample and a rhythm with an incredibly straight-sounding hi-hat part drive the track, and eventually, a chorus becomes apparent. The simple half-step chord change up and back again halfway through is like a mini version of Miles Davis' classic chord progression from 'So What'.

Though 'The One' bears no hallmarks of the EW&F sound besides vocals), as with 'Work It Out', the listener is in for a pleasurable experience.

'Elevated' (Ambrosius, Stewart, Henson, Pelzer)

From its very beginning, 'Elevated' will make fans of top-tier singing very happy. Natalie Stewart and Marsha Ambrosius made up the popular British duo Floetry, whose smash 2005 album *Flo'Ology* debuted at seven on the Billboard 200. Stewart and Ambrosius wrote the song with producers Darren Henson and Keith Pelzer (both fresh off the success of Jill Scott's *Beautifully Human: Words And Sounds Vol. 2*), and they also worked on *Flo'Ology*. Bailey blends with the duo marvellously, and Natalie Stewart raps in the verse, occasionally augmented by Ambrosius. The pre-chorus features smooth vocals from Ambrosius, Bailey weaving around her melodies. The chorus is lush and filled to the brim with vocal talent, topped off with a sparkling-clean sound. 'Don't let go/Don't you know/You'll be alright/Ease your mind/Elevated', the blended vocals call out to the listener, though it's all washed away with the arrival of verse two. The second pre-chorus contains some absolutely stunning notes from Bailey.

The only complaint is that 'Elevate' perhaps sounds more like Bailey guesting on a Floetry track rather than the other way around.

'Liberation' (Duplaix, Bervine)

DJ Vikter Duplaix makes his *Illumination* contribution with 'Liberation' – a co-write with Junius Bervine. Duplaix made his name with his 2002 solo album *International Affairs*, and a year after the release of *Illumination*, his song 'Make A Baby' was nominated for a Grammy in the Best Urban/ Alternative Performance category. Bervine became a successful producer, working with artists such as Pharrell and Common.

A promising synth introduction is layered with sounds of birds and running water and birds to begin: a mystical feeling. Then a horse-like percussion section makes the groove, Verdine hitting some of his much-missed vibrato bass notes. A percussive turn is taken as the track strips down, Verdine still hanging in there tight. Duplaix's work with Incognito and Jamiroquai comes to mind here in the dance groove. Myron McKinley's sparkling piano licks add an air of sophistication.

'Liberation' takes the proud tradition of instrumental numbers that EW&F established in the 1970s, and brings it into the (at the time) present day, almost working better than it feels like it should. It's an excellent contribution from Duplaix and Bervine.

'To You' (McKnight)

Popular soul singer/producer and television personality Brian McKnight produced and wrote 'To You'. As the album's final single, it reached 16 on the Adult R&B chart and 29 Smooth Jazz Songs. Filling the obligatory ballad role on the album, the track opens with piano – as the group's adult-contemporary tracks are prone to. McKnight soon begins to croon a tale of love – 'Don't try to hide the way you feel/'Cause deep inside you know you can feel it', giving off shades of Luther Vandross in the process. The verse eventually moves to the pre-chorus and the mid-tempo rhythm. Bailey and McKnight's voices work well together, enhancing the track before leaning into the smooth, silky chorus. Maurice comes in for the second chorus, backing vocals building a tower of sound underneath his hooks. The second chorus is as splendid as the first, and the group quote themselves in the turnaround to the bridge – the 'woah oh oh ohhh' that helped make 'After The Love Has Gone' so special, rearing its head once more, though quickly, for keen listeners. The final chorus finds Maurice bringing in a new hook, and 'To You' fades into the night not long after.

'The Way You Move' (Brown, Patton, Mahone Jr.)
Ending the album is the lead single – a cover of the Outkast hit 'The Way You Move', with smooth-jazz saxophonist Kenny G. Originally released the year before on Kenny G's *At Last…The Duets* album, the track also tied into *Illumination* in a clever cross-promotion. Recorded with Kenny's longtime producer Walter Afanasieff and Raphael Saadiq, the track is a reasonable, smooth jazz reworking of the original. Kenny's sax intones the original vocal melody, the EW&F element mainly coming in the chorus backing vocals, though Bailey does take the lead for the second verse. Maurice's bridge vocal is notable, and 'The Way You Move' is a great little cover, even if its inclusion brings nothing special in particular. The single reached 12 on the Adult Contemporary chart.

Now, Then & Forever (2013)

Personnel:
Philip Bailey: vocals, congas, percussion
Ralph Johnson: drums, percussion, vocals
Verdine White: bass, percussion, vocals
Philip Doron Bailey: vocals
John Paris: drums
Morris O'Connor: lead guitar
Serg Dimitrijevic: rhythm guitar
David B. Butterworth: percussion, vocals
Myron McKinley: keyboards
Gary Bias, Mark Visher: saxophone
Additional Musicians:
Reggie Young, Eric Jorgenson, Wendell Kelly, Nicholas Lane: trombone
Chuck Findley, Terence Blanchard, Sal Cracchiolo, Christopher Grey, John Pappenbrook, James Ford III, Mathew Fronke: trumpet
Errol Cooney, Gregory Moore, Jairus Mozee: guitar
Producers: Philip Bailey, Jai-Dig, Neal H. Pogue, Walt B, Lee Hutson Jr., Justin Panariello, Philip Doron Bailey, Larry Dunn
Executive producer: Philip Bailey
Mixing: Neal H. Pogue, Dave Pensado
Engineers: David Rideao, Eric Rousseau, Justin Merill, Kenny Moran, Paul Klingberg
Mastering: Brian Gardner at Record Technology Unlimited
Studios: Blakeslee, Dunn-Elliot, Launchpad, Mungo Bungo, NRG, NuVintage, The Alcove, California; Germano Studios, New York
Release date: 21 October 2013
Chart positions: US: 11, 6 (R&B), UK: 25
Running time: 43:29 sh

Earth, Wind & Fire headed back to the studio for their last album of all-original material to this date. Under the guidance of Bailey, they looked to make a fully-fledged return to their original sound, albeit without Maurice for the first time. His health had declined to the point where he could no longer work in the studio or otherwise, and his last EW&F contribution was the following open letter included in the album booklet:

As we see today's technology uniting the world wide web, sometimes it seems that the hearts of men are growing more distant from each other. It is my hope that this music will continue to tie the past to the future, reminding us of the love that united us to our ancestors, and to our descendants, and to each other. Peace, Maurice White.

Along with the intrigue of hearing EW&F without its longtime leader, fans might also have been encouraged to purchase the album due to the huge news of Larry Dunn's return. Dunn would contribute his legendary synth sounds, and worked on songwriting and production. Bailey told the *Fayetteville Observer*: 'I said, 'Let's go back to the drawing board'. It's a great representation of who Earth, Wind & Fire is now, but not departing from the classic sound'. Another change came in the form of Bailey's son Philip Doran Bailey helping with production and backing vocals, Bailey also saying, 'It's a great experience to say the least. I spend so much time away from my family and kids that this is bonding like never before. He has the same passion'.

To achieve the result Bailey was looking for, numerous songwriters were again employed. Lee Hutson Jr. – son of legendary American soul vocalist Leroy Hutson – was called on. The album was a critical and commercial success, reaching 11 in the US. Verdine recalled the album's impact in a 2016 interview with *Time Out* magazine: 'Producer Neal Pogue who worked with Outkast, did a marvellous job. He was so in tune with us. We thought that we could go back to our roots. We were pleasantly surprised that we sounded great just like that. That was really fantastic'.

'Sign On' (Bailey, Simpson, Pogue, McClain, Gibson, Jacobs)
Within seconds, 'Sign On' establishes itself as brimming over with the signature EW&F sound. The new guitar team of Morris O'Connor and Serg Dimitrijevic are also noticeable, locking in through the chord changes. Bailey opens the song, and after a couple of lines, soul singer Daniel Skyhigh McClain takes over, sounding like silk on top of the hard rhythm. McClain later worked with Steven Tyler, Lalah Hathaway and others, and his work here really stands out. Bailey and McClain blend for the pre-chorus, raising the track's dynamic in the process. The lyric is deeper and more thoughtful than most tracks across the last few albums:

Every time we seem to look around
I can see the people crying out
'Cause the fear, hate and power
And that good ol' mighty dollar
Time to unite and make it right within us

It's certainly a more powerful opening statement than the will.i.am-penned 'Lovely People' on *Illumination*.

The chorus works incredibly well, the hook beginning with a strong high note before tumbling down the scale. Strong and memorable, the band here sound refreshed. Verdine puts in what may be his best work since 1982, coming alive and keeping the track turning. The smooth, sci-fi-esque jazz chords of the bridge movement truly sound like prime-era EW&F, and the singers remain long after the music has faded away, reinforcing the message.

'Sign On' is the way to open an EW&F album, and the group sounds more like themselves than they had in years. The only regret is that this didn't

119

occur while Maurice was capable of performing, though his blessing in the
included booklet does make that fact easier to swallow.

'Love Is Law' (Hutson Jr., Todd, Rousseau, Key, Bundy, Mozee)

'Love Is Law' keeps up the high quality, and features a stiff neo-soul rhythm
for the band to play around. Relaxing chord changes give Bailey a platform to
begin vocal – 'In love we live, in love you breathe/If love you give, then love
received'. Larry Dunn's playing is an absolute pleasure to hear again, giving the
sound a distinct flavour of his own, and always playing for the song's benefit.
Philip Doren Bailey joins McClain for the chorus backing vocals, Bailey taking
centre stage with a passionate performance. The chorus constantly builds and
is instantly memorable. Bailey's presence really boosts the track, giving keen-
eared listeners some interesting countermelodies to focus on. Rather than
having a written bridge, the track is stripped back for Verdine's busy playing
with the horn section, culminating in the return of the chorus.

'Love Is Law' is another knockout blow, giving *Now Then & Forever* a good,
stomping groove.

'My Promise' (Jacobs, Simpson, Garrett)

'My Promise' couldn't be mistaken for anything but Earth, Wind & Fire as
soon as the horn intro begins, the mix giving the horns a top-end boost that
makes the track really pop. Songwriters Austin Jacobs (who later worked on
America's Got Talent), Darrin Simpson and Siedah Garrett (Madonna, Michael
Jackson, Brand New Heavies) really bring the essence of EW&F to the track –
their knowledge of what makes the group tick, evident in the song itself.

Bailey sings in a low register to begin the verse, even throwing in a
couple of Maurice-like 'well's for good measure. As with the previous tracks,
the melody is impactful and memorable. The chorus finds the vocals picking
up, with McClain and the younger Bailey filling the track with luscious
harmonies alongside Siedah Garrett's sweet tone. The bridge features an
excellent new set of chords, Bailey hitting an incredible note to signal
the section's end. The chorus is repeated to the end, by this time firmly
imprinted in the listener's mind.

'My Promise' isn't just a great modern EW&F track, it's a great EW&F track
full-stop. Released as the album's second single, it reached 28 on the Adult
R&B chart, and 30 on Adult Contemporary Songs.

'Guiding Lights' (Bailey, Jacobs, Simpson, McClain)

The lead single brings the album down low, burning with a smouldering
passion and bringing a truly epic vibe. It reached 16 on the Smooth Jazz
Songs chart and 30 Adult R&B.

Dunn's presence is really felt here, his striking synth sounds starting the
track in style. Bailey's voice glides through the atmosphere established by the
group. The pre-chorus takes things up a notch with some horn lines jolting

back and forth, as does the chorus with the arrival of the backing vocals. An accented turnaround guides them back to the slow rocking verse groove.

Bailey brings it up for the second verse, reaching for the stars and sounding great as usual, and the second chorus keeps up the ethereal mood. Dunn counters the bridge melody with his signature sounds before soloing. Bailey helps him bring the section to a pinnacle, before the chorus again rolls around. Dunn stretches out here with some hot fusion licks: showing why he's been so sorely missed.

'Got To Be Love' (Bailey, Bailey, Johnson, McKinley)
Written with musical director Myron McKinley, 'Got To Be Love' features a sneaky groove constantly looking around corners, bringing to mind the riffs of D'Angelo. The guitar and bass lock in tight with the drums of John Paris. A blast of Dunn's keys opens the door for the verse, Bailey again singing in the vocal area Maurice usually occupied. The riff hangs tight for the chorus, Bailey playing off the backing vocals in the same low register. Rather than the expected next chorus, we get an extended guitar solo from O'Connor, who keeps it soulful. This eventually dissolves into some beautiful piano from Dunn as the track winds down.

'Belo Horizonte' (Johnson, O'Connor, Crossley, Johnson)
Running at just under two minutes, 'Belo Horizonte' is a detour into Latin jazz, and the group sound great doing it. Dunn's synth lines bring an extra dimension, while percussion holds down the rhythm for O'Connor and Dimitrijevic to lay down some lovely nylon acoustic guitar.

'Dance Floor' (Bailey, Bailey, Panariello)
A thumping four-on-the-floor groove opens 'Dance Floor', before Verdine's instantly-recognizable bass tone appears. An auto-tuned Ralph Johnson opens the verse with a monotone melody before Bailey takes over. This pattern is repeated for the rest of the verse. The snare keeps doubling in speed (a popular method in EDM drum fills) before exploding into the chorus, an interesting descending chord sequence and catchy melody being the staples of the section. This all repeats, the second chorus punctuated by Dunn's synth before a remarkable horn and vocal line leaves the listener stunned with its be bop-like complexity. Some rhythmic vocal parts from Bailey reverberate around the mix with delay, before the chorus appears augmented by a new melody from Dunn. The track eventually breaks down into some funky guitar chords and Verdine's riff, before abruptly ending.

'Splashes' (Bailey, Panariello)
Essentially a modern-jazz track, 'Splashes' has echoes of The Pat Metheny Group's recordings from around the early-1990s (see the album *Letters From Home* for example). Cymbals wash over the listener, the vocal lines mixed low

to draw them in. Terence Blanchard's trumpet occasionally pierces through the web, breaking the trance. Dunn's soundscape envelops the listener, creating a whole world to explore.

'Splashes' helps re-establish the group's jazz prowess, and sounds fresh and modern in the process, pushing the envelope into a new direction that would've been good to hear more of. The tabla-playing of Satnam Singh Ramgotra should also be noted.

'Night Of My Life' (Bailey, McGlory, Panariello)
'Night Of My Life' is a disco barn burner right away. A two-note guitar/horn line hooks the listener before Bailey begins his vocal line. The chorus has rock overtones with its distorted guitar, and Bailey puts in a meaningful performance.

It's by no means a bad track, but something about the drum sound holds it back from being as full-bodied as the others and leaves the mix feeling slightly empty.

'The Rush' (Bailey, Willis, Dunn)
Maurice's shadow looms over this song during the kalimba intro (played by Bailey), before a deep 12/8 groove begins. Bailey's high melody is unusual, broken up by syncopated horn lines, before he goes low for the last half of the verse: showing his one-of-a-kind vocal range. The group are really swinging in the pre-chorus, a great guitar and bass riff peaking through the vocal. A modified blues progression is established for the chorus, suiting the groove to a tee, while Bailey sings a hook that's sure to stay with the listener long after listening. The track closes with the post-chorus groove, Dunn's sweet organ loud in the mix.

'The Rush' is a great ending to the album, establishing the group's mature funk before ending in an explosion. *Now, Then & Forever* ends as it began: on a high note.

Holiday (2014)

Personnel:
Maurice White: vocals, drums, kalimba, percussion
Ralph Johnson: drums, percussion, vocals
Philip Bailey: vocals, congas, percussion
Verdine White: bass, percussion, vocals
Philip Doren Bailey: vocals
John Paris: drums
Morris O'Connor: lead guitar
Serg Dimitrijevic: rhythm guitar
David B. Butterworth: percussion, vocals
Myron McKinley: keyboards, piano, synthersizer
Jerry Peters: organ
Gary Bias: saxophone
Gary Grant: trumpet
Reggie Young: trombone
Producers: Philip Bailey, Myron McKinlay, Philip Doran Bailey
Mixing: Dave Pensado
Engineers: Dave Pensado, Jimmi Randolph, Paul Klingberg, Tommy Vicari, Gus Pirelli
Mastering: Brian Gardner at Bernie Grundman Mastering
Studios: NRG, Mungo Bungo, Sound Temple, LAFX, Capitol, Music Box, California
Release date: 21 October 2014
Chart positions: US: 8 (Holiday), 26 (R&B), UK: -
Running time: 47:28

After the return to form of *Now, Then & Forever,* Sony looked to capitalise on the group's comeback by having them release a holiday album. *Holiday* was released precisely a year after *Now, Then & Forever*, and featured the group reinterpreting holiday classics in their own funky style, as well as giving the Christmas treatment to some of their own hits. Whether the world truly needed this following such a return to form, could be disputed, but we have it anyway, waiting to be pulled out once a year to avoid more-saccharine versions of classic Christmas tunes. Verdine told *Billboard*: 'It's our special twist. We never thought about doing a holiday album before, but Sony/Legacy asked and so have our fans, so we hope the audience like it'. Bailey commented in the same interview: 'We stretched the envelope a bit on several songs, changing the harmonic structures and rhythms – kind of like what we did with 'Got To Get You Into My Life'. It's Christmas songs, but still Earth, Wind & Fire-esque'.

The album definitely pulled the songs in new directions, but it can't be recommended for listening over any of the group's original studio albums, and feels like a bit too much of a novelty to be taken seriously.

Holiday is to date the group's last collection of recordings: ending their studio career on a light note. Sadly, Maurice White passed away peacefully in his sleep on 4 February 2016: less than two years after the album's release. He will be remembered as a towering musician, a provider of some of the biggest hits, and one of the finest bandleaders. Verdine released a statement via the group's social media channels:

> My brother, hero and best friend Maurice White, passed away peacefully last night in his sleep. While the world has lost another great musician and legend, our family asks that our privacy is respected as we start what will be a very difficult and life-changing transition in our lives. Thank you for your prayers and well wishes.

Perhaps it's fitting that the group ceased to release music after this album, right before the death of the man who carried the group's torch high and proud for so many years.

'Joy To The World' (Watts)
This funky take on the Christmas carol has little in common with the well-known composition, and the up-tempo rhythm is complemented by Bailey mainly talking in response to the gospel choir. There are snatches of both the original melody and the burning EW&F horn lines throughout. Bailey's incredible runs are the highlight – his dexterity is still mind-blowing after all these years. Morris O'Connor takes a bluesy solo, slowly building in intensity as the track fades.

'Happy Seasons' (White, Bailey, White, McKay, Dunn)
A new take on the *That's The Way of The World* classic, this one sticks pretty close to the original, with an updated lyric to fit the holiday theme. The production is obviously updated, and Bailey again proves he hasn't lost a step. It's a fun romp through a classic, though the original is superior.

'O' Come All Ye Faithful' (Wade, Reading)
Here we find Bailey crooning through a faithful rendition. Guitar strums gently behind while the group experiments with re-harmonising, to squeeze some new life into the song – mournful strings adding to the mood. Myron McKinley's piano solo is a highlight.

'Winter Wonderland' (Bernard)
If a disco take on 'Winter Wonderland' is what you need to get your Christmas party started, then this is what you've been waiting for. Horns are studded along the chords, and Bailey goes back and forth with the thick backing vocals, altering the rhythm of the lyric in favour of a soulful, syncopated take. The band sound as tight as ever delivering the funky arrangement.

'What Child is This?' (Dix)

A sprawling string section begins with a sweeping intro before a thumping kick and percussion bring in the groove proper. Horns bounce off the guitar chords, and the strings shine throughout. The mysterious chord changes give a moody feeling, as opposed to the usual Christmas cheer. 'What Child Is This?' is one of the album's more-interesting tracks.

'Away In A Manger' (Murray)

This interpolates the opening horn/vocal riff from the group's classic *All 'N All* soul stirrer 'Be Ever Wonderful'. It moves along nicely like most of the album but doesn't offer much to remember besides the group's use of old-school melody.

'The Little Drummer Boy' (Simeone, Davis)

This is reworked via a Bo Diddley-style groove with acoustic guitar. The melody is faithful to the original, which may be a good gauge as to the need of the listener to hear this take.

'Every Day Is Like Christmas' (Steinke, Seeman)

This cheerful is a crooning jazz bop for Bailey to show his mastery of the genre. Perhaps this angle might've worked well for the whole album – the group sounding comfortable with the jazz surroundings, while offering something a little different.

'The First Noel' (Gilbert, Sandys)

Another Christmas standard, with reworked chord changes and a funky groove. Again, the listener's enjoyment may depend on their love of Christmas or prior interest in the song.

'Sleigh Ride' (Anderson)

'Sleigh Ride' retrieves the original groove and progression of 'Sing A Song', with the sleigh-based lyric. There's a whiff of musical theatre in the track, particularly in the 'Giddy up, giddy up' vocal section. But otherwise, there's not much here that's different to the rest of the album.

'Snow' (Trad. Japanese)

This upbeat interpretation of the traditional Japanese piece finds vocalist Suzie Katayama duetting with Philip. The big guitar and synth chord changes bring to mind Prince's work around the *Planet Earth* era, but the saccharine melody may be too much for those not in the mood for Christmas cheer.

'Jingle Bell Rock' (Boothe, Beal)

This undisputed classic gets a reasonably faithful rendition here, with re-harmonising to keep the listener engaged. Driven by funky guitar rhythms, the horns really punch out, and Bailey again adopts a low croon. It's a nice, easygoing version of the well-known song.

'December' (White, McKay, Willis)
Upon reading the song title of the closing track, you can predict what's in store, and it is indeed an updated version of 'September', with an eye on the Christmas market. Rather pointless as a listening exercise, it's most likely aimed at getting spins in shopping malls. The only interesting feature is Maurice's original vocal track being dusted off and used to duet with Bailey. It's a predictable ending to a fairly-predictable album.

Live Albums and Compilations

Earth, Wind & Fire have a rich trail of compilations (beginning with the already-covered *The Best of Earth, Wind & Fire, Vol. 1*), and great live albums that have been released years after the event. For the sake of saving the reader from endless retreads, only the most important compilations will be covered, and only official releases in regard to live albums.

'The Best Of Earth, Wind & Fire, Vol. 2' (1988)
This companion album to 'Vol. 1' (1978) picks up where that left off, mopping up the group's remaining hits. The album opens with the rarity 'Turn On (The Beat Box)' – an upbeat, poppy track originally found on the soundtrack of the hit 1988 film *Caddyshack II* (Fans of the *Touch The World* era will enjoy this one). Other than that, classics such as 'After The Love Has Gone', 'Devotion' and 'Boogie Wonderland' can be found right here for casual 1980s fans and those looking to re-familiarise themselves with the catalogue before diving into *Touch The World*.

'The Eternal Dance' (1992)
This three-disc box set covers the group's career up to the point of its release. To satisfy the more hardcore fan, there are rarities sprinkled throughout – mainly in the form of outtakes, alternate versions and live tracks. The unreleased 'Night Dreamin'' is the real gem here – a forgotten track from 1982. Sweet strings and funky guitar abound, with a broad, sweeping chorus and a great horn arrangement. The brief and simply titled 'Demo' gives a glimpse behind the curtain into Maurice' working style.

Constellations: The Universe of Earth, Wind & Fire (2012)
This streaming-only compilation is essentially a modern update of *The Eternal Dance*, and includes multiple live tracks, alternative mixes, edits and instrumental. The 1987 smooth jazz outtake 'Eyes Of Hope' is included for completists, as is the straight-up 1980s pop track 'Insensitive'. Dunn's work with Caldera appears in the form of 'Seraphim', along with Maurice's work on Barbra Streisand's 'Time Machine'. *Constellations* does its best to mix things up, and is a good guide to the group's work, as opposed to a traditional greatest hits.

Live in Rio (2002)
Recorded live in Rio de Janeiro, Brazil, in 1980, highlights include a fiery run through 'Serpentine Fire', and the instrumental jam 'Rio After Dark', during which the band flash their fusion chops to great effect. A remarkable live document from the band at the top of their game.

Live in Japan (1999)
Released with a DVD companion, this finds the group live during the tour for

Heritage. Despite what the listener may think of the group during this era, they're in fine live form.

Greatest Hits Live (1998)

Frequently re-packaged, this can also be found under the titles *Plugged in and Live* and *Live in Velfarre*. It's well worth tracking down, again featuring the group live in Japan, this time at The Velfarre, Tokyo, in 1995.